to:

from:

date:

FAMILY
Christian Stores

uys > girls and guys > girls a

WHY ME?

100 Days of Answers

teen SERIES

devos

s > girls and guys > girls and

FAMILY CHRISTIAN STORES
Grand Rapids, MI 49530

The quoted ideas expressed in this book (but not scripture verses) are not, in all cases, exact quotations, as some have been edited for clarity and brevity. In all cases, the author has attempted to maintain the speaker's original intent. In some cases, quoted material for this book was obtained from secondary sources, primarily print media. While every effort was made to ensure the accuracy of these sources, the accuracy cannot be guaranteed. For additions, deletions, corrections or clarifications in future editions of this text, please write FAMILY CHRISTIAN STORES.

Cover Design by Kim Russell / Wahoo Designs
Page Layout by Bart Dawson

ISBN 978-1-60587-063-2

Printed in the United States of America

guys > girls and guys > girls a

WHY ME?

100 Days of Answers

teen SERIES devos

s > girls and guys > girls and

Introduction

Why me? It's a one of many questions that you may find easier to ask than to answer. And this book can help you sort things out. On the pages that follow, you'll find real answers—God's answers—to the questions that many young men and women ask.

As you know from firsthand experience, it isn't easy being a young person in our 21st-century world. Every day, you are confronted with countless opportunities to wander away from the path that God intends for you to take. Every day, you come face-to-face with questions, temptations, and distractions that were unknown to previous generations. Every day, you have difficult choices to make—choices that can help you become the person God wants you be . . . or not. And make no mistake: the results of your choices will have far-reaching consequences.

This book contains 100 brief devotional readings that are intended to help you figure out the answers to some of the questions you may have been asking yourself. Are you facing difficult decisions? Are you seeking to change some aspect of your life? Do you want to gain a better understanding of the person you are and the person you can be in the future? If so, ask for God's help and ask for it many times each day . . . starting with a regular, heartfelt morning devotional. When you do, you will change your day . . . and your life.

Today's Big Question About Tough Times

Question:

During tough times, what should you do?

Answer:

When tough times arrive, you should work as if everything depended on you and pray as if everything depended on God.

It's a promise that is made over and over again in the Bible: Whatever "it" is, God can handle it.

Life isn't always easy. Far from it! Sometimes, life can be very, very tough. But even then, even during our darkest moments, we're protected by a loving Heavenly Father. When we're worried, God can reassure us; when we're sad, God can comfort us. When our hearts are broken, God is not just near; He is here. So we must lift our thoughts and prayers to Him. When we do, He will answer our prayers. Why? Because He is our Shepherd, and He has promised to protect us now and forever.

Give your burdens to the Lord, and he will take care of you. He will not permit the godly to slip and fall.

Psalm 55:22 NLT

Your greatest ministry will likely come out of your greatest hurt.

Rick Warren

You may not know what you are going to do; you only know that God knows what He is going to do.

Oswald Chambers

Jesus does not say, "There is no storm." He says, "I am here, do not toss, but trust."

Vance Havner

Talk about it . . . If you're having tough times, don't hit the panic button and don't keep everything bottled up inside. Talk things over with your friends or your parents, and if necessary, find a counselor you can really trust. A second opinion (or, for that matter, a third, fourth, or fifth opinion) is usually helpful. So if your troubles seem overwhelming, be willing to seek outside help.

Day 2

Today's Big Question About God's Answers

Question:

Life can be tough to figure out. Where can I go to the find the answers I need?

Answer:

If you have questions, God has answers. So talk to Him often and study His Word every day.

So many questions and so few answers! If that statement seems to describe the current state of your spiritual life, don't panic. Even the most faithful Christians are overcome by occasional bouts of fear and doubt. You are no different.

When you feel that your faith is being tested to its limits, seek the comfort and assurance of the One who sent His Son as a sacrifice for you. And remember: Even when you feel very distant from God, God is never distant from you. When you sincerely seek His presence, He will touch your heart, calm your fears, and give you the strength to meet any challenge,

Now if any of you lacks wisdom, he should ask God, who gives to all generously and without criticizing, and it will be given to him. But let him ask in faith without doubting. For the doubter is like the surging sea, driven and tossed by the wind.

James 1:5-6 HCSB

When there is perplexity there is always guidance—not always at the moment we ask, but in good time, which is God's time. There is no need to fret and stew.

Elisabeth Elliot

We are finding we don't have such a gnawing need to know the answers when we know the Answer.

Gloria Gaither

Be to the world a sign that while we as Christians do not have all the answers, we do know and care about the questions.

Billy Graham

Too many questions? If you're faced with too many questions and too few answers, talk to God about it. When you do, you'll discover that He has more answers than you have questions.

Day 3

Today's Big Question About Fear

Question:

Sometimes, the world can be a scary place. What does the Bible say about fear?

Answer:

If you're feeling fearful or anxious, you must trust God to solve the problems that are simply too big for you to solve.

We live in a world that is, at times, a frightening place. We live in a world that is, at times, a discouraging place. We live in a world where life-changing losses can be so painful and so profound that it seems we will never recover. But, with God's help, and with the help of encouraging family members and friends, we can recover.

During the darker days of life, we are wise to remember the words of Jesus, who reassured His disciples, saying, "Take courage! It is I. Don't be afraid" (Matthew 14:27 NIV). Then, with God's comfort and His love in our hearts, we can offer encouragement to others. And by helping them face their fears, we can, in turn, tackle our own problems with courage, determination, and faith.

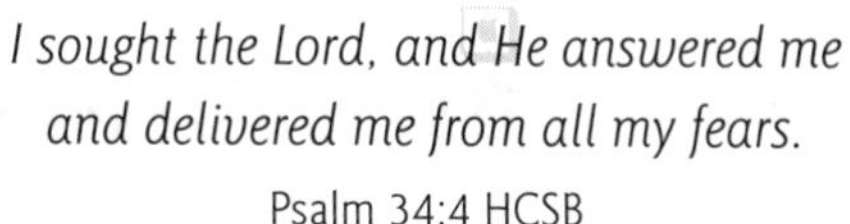

I sought the Lord, and He answered me
and delivered me from all my fears.

Psalm 34:4 HCSB

When we meditate on God and remember
the promises He has given us in His Word,
our faith grows, and our fears dissolve.

Charles Stanley

The Lord Jesus by His Holy Spirit is with me,
and the knowledge of His presence dispels
the darkness and allays any fears.

Bill Bright

When once we are assured that God is good,
then there can be nothing left to fear.

Hannah Whitall Smith

A Prayer: Your Word reminds me, Lord, that even when I walk through the valley of the shadow of death, I need fear no evil, for You are with me, and You comfort me. Thank You, Lord, for a perfect love that casts out fear. Let me live courageously and faithfully this day and every day. Amen

Day 4

Today's Big Question About Discipline

Question:
What does the Bible say about discipline?

Answer:
Time and again, the Bible praises discipline. A disciplined lifestyle gives you more control: The more disciplined you become, the more you can take control over your life (which, by the way, is far better than letting your life take control over you).

Sometimes, it's hard to be dignified and disciplined. Why? Because you live in a world where many prominent people want you to believe that dignified, self-disciplined behavior is going out of style. But don't kid yourself: self-discipline never goes out of style.

Face facts: Life's greatest rewards aren't likely to fall into your lap. To the contrary, your greatest accomplishments will probably require plenty of work and a heaping helping of self-discipline—which, by the way, is perfectly fine with God. After all, He knows that you're up to the task, and He has big plans for you. God will do His part to fulfill those plans, and the rest, of course, depends upon you.

So prepare your minds for service and have self-control. All your hope should be for the gift of grace that will be yours when Jesus Christ is shown to you.

I Peter 1:13 NCV

Personal humility is a spiritual discipline and the hallmark of the service of Jesus.

Franklin Graham

If one examines the secret behind a championship football team, a magnificent orchestra, or a successful business, the principal ingredient is invariably discipline.

James Dobson

No horse gets anywhere until he is harnessed. No life ever grows great until it is focused, dedicated, disciplined.

Harry Emerson Fosdick

A disciplined lifestyle gives you more control: The more disciplined you become, the more you can take control over your life (which, by the way, is far better than letting your life take control over you).

Day 5

Today's Big Question About Accepting Christ

Question:

What does the Bible say about the kind of relationship that I should establish with Jesus Christ?

Answer:

It is critically important to be certain that you have welcomed Christ into your heart. If you've accepted Christ, congratulations. If not, the time to accept Him is now!

Your decision to allow Christ to reign over your heart is the pivotal decision of your life. It is a decision that you cannot ignore. It is a decision that is yours and yours alone.

God's love for you is deeper and more profound than you can imagine. God's love for you is so great that He sent His only Son to this earth to die for your sins and to offer you the priceless gift of eternal life. Now, you must decide whether or not to accept God's gift. Will you ignore it or embrace it? Will you return it or neglect it? Will you accept Christ's love and build a lifelong relationship with Him, or will you turn away from Him and take a different path?

Accept God's gift now: allow His Son to preside over your heart, your thoughts, and your life, starting this very instant.

For God so loved the world that he gave his one and only Son, that whoever believes in him shall not perish but have eternal life.

John 3:16 NIV

Evidence of new birth is that we see the rule of God.

Oswald Chambers

It's your heart that Jesus longs for: your will to be made His own with self on the cross forever, and Jesus alone on the throne.

Ruth Bell Graham

The amount of power you experience to live a victorious, triumphant Christian life is directly proportional to the freedom you give the Spirit to be Lord of your life!

Anne Graham Lotz

It is critically important to be certain that you have welcomed Christ into your heart. If you've accepted Christ, congratulations. If not, the time to accept Him is now!

Day 6

Today's Big Question About Your Daily Devotional

Question:

It isn't always easy to find time to study your Bible every day. What does God expect you to do?

Answer:

He wants you to get reacquainted with Him every day: No exceptions!

Want to hold things together and feel better about your world? Then schedule a meeting with God every day.

Daily life is a tapestry of habits, and no habit is more important to your spiritual health than the discipline of daily prayer and devotion to the Creator. When you begin each day with your head bowed and your heart lifted, you are reminded of God's love and God's laws.

When you do engage in a regular regime of worship and praise, God will reward you for your wisdom and your obedience. Each new day is a gift from God, and if you're wise, you'll spend a few quiet moments thanking the Giver. It's a wonderful way to start your day.

Morning by morning he wakens me and opens
my understanding to his will.
The Sovereign Lord has spoken to me, and I have listened.

Isaiah 50:4-5 NLT

Maintenance of the devotional mood is indispensable to success in the Christian life.

A. W. Tozer

The moment you wake up each morning, all your wishes and hopes for the day rush at you like wild animals. And the first job each morning consists in shoving it all back; in listening to that other voice, taking that other point of view, letting that other, larger, stronger, quieter life coming flowing in.

C. S. Lewis

A person with no devotional life generally struggles with faith and obedience.

Charles Stanley

Make an appointment with God and keep it. Bible study and prayer should be at the top of your to-do list, not the bottom.

Day 7

Today's Big Question About Courage

Question:

Sometimes life is tough. When you're afraid, what should you do?

Answer:

Turn things over to God. Courage is trusting God to handle the problems that are simply too big for you to solve.

Every life (including yours) is an unfolding series of events: some fabulous, some not-so-fabulous, and some downright disheartening. When you reach the mountaintops of life, praising God is easy. But, when the storm clouds form overhead, your faith will be tested, sometimes to the breaking point. As a believer, you can take comfort in this fact: Wherever you find yourself, whether at the top of the mountain or the depths of the valley, God is there, and because He cares for you, you can live courageously.

Believing Christians have every reason to be courageous. After all, the ultimate battle has already been fought and won on the cross at Calvary. But, even dedicated followers of Christ may find their courage tested by the inevitable disappointments and tragedies that occur in the lives of believers and non-believers alike.

The next time you find your courage tested to the limit, remember that God is as near as your next breath, and remember that He is your shield and your strength; He is your protector and your deliverer. Call upon Him in your hour of need and then be comforted. Whatever your challenge, whatever your trouble, God can handle it. And will.

Be strong and courageous, and do the work.
Don't be afraid or discouraged, for the Lord God, my God,
is with you. He won't leave you or forsake you.

I Chronicles 28:20 HCSB

When once we are assured that God is good,
then there can be nothing left to fear.

Hannah Whitall Smith

God of grace and God of glory, on Thy people pour
Thy power. Grant us wisdom; grant us courage
for the facing of this hour.

Harry Emerson Fosdick

Do not let Satan deceive you into being afraid of God's plans for your life.

Day 8

Today's Big Question About Change

Question:

Your world is changing faster and faster. What should you do?

Answer:

If a big change is called for . . . don't be afraid to make a big change—sometimes, one big leap is better than a thousand baby steps.

We live in a world that is always changing, but we worship a God that never changes—thank goodness! That means that we can be comforted in the knowledge that our Heavenly Father is the rock that simply cannot be moved: "I am the Lord, I do not change" (Malachi 3:6 NKJV).

The next time you face difficult circumstances, tough times, unfair treatment, or unwelcome changes, remember that some things never change—things like the love that you feel in your heart for your family and friends . . . and the love that God feels for you. So, instead of worrying too much about life's inevitable challenges, focus your energies on finding solutions. Have faith in your own abilities, do your best to solve your problems, and leave the rest up to God.

There is a time for everything, and a season for every activity under heaven.

Ecclesiastes 3:1 NIV

With God, it isn't who you were that matters; it's who you are becoming.

Liz Curtis Higgs

The secret of contentment in the midst of change is found in having roots in the changeless Christ—the same yesterday, today and forever.

Ed Young

Conditions are always changing; therefore, I must not be dependent upon conditions. What matters supremely is my soul and my relationship to God.

Corrie ten Boom

The world continues to change, as do you. Change is inevitable—you can either roll with it or be rolled over by it. In order to avoid the latter, you should choose the former . . . and trust God as you go.

Day 9

Today's Big Question About Listening to Your Conscience

Question:

What does the Bible say about following your conscience?

Answer:

That quiet little voice inside your head will guide you down the right path if you listen carefully. Very often, your conscience will actually tell you what God wants you to do. So listen, learn, and behave accordingly.

Billy Graham correctly observed, "Most of us follow our conscience as we follow a wheelbarrow. We push it in front of us in the direction we want to go." To do so, of course, is a profound mistake. Yet all of us, on occasion, have failed to listen to the voice that God planted in our hearts, and all of us have suffered the consequences.

God gave you a conscience for a very good reason: to make your path conform to His will. Wise believers make it a practice to listen carefully to that quiet internal voice. Count yourself among that number. When your conscience speaks, listen and learn. In all likelihood, God is trying to get His message through. And in all likelihood, it is a message that you desperately need to hear.

Now the goal of our instruction is love from a pure heart, a good conscience, and a sincere faith.

I Timothy 1:5 HCSB

God desires that we become spiritually healthy enough through faith to have a conscience that rightly interprets the work of the Holy Spirit.

Beth Moore

To go against one's conscience is neither safe nor right. Here I stand. I cannot do otherwise.

Martin Luther

The convicting work of the Holy Spirit awakens, disturbs, and judges.

Franklin Graham

A good conscience is a continual feast.

Francis Bacon

The more important the decision . . . the more carefully you should listen to your conscience.

Day 10

Today's Big Question About Bitterness

Question:

Why is it important to overcome feelings of bitterness?

Answer:

Because feelings of bitterness and hate are destructive. And besides, the Bible commands you to forgive other people.

If you're unwilling to forgive other people, you're building a roadblock between yourself and God. And the less you're willing to forgive, the bigger your roadblock. So if you want to know God in a more meaningful way, you must learn how to forgive and, to the best of your abilities, forget.

Is there someone out there you need to forgive? If so, pray for that person. And then pray for yourself by asking God to heal your heart. Don't expect forgiveness to be easy or quick, but rest assured: with God as your partner, you can forgive . . . and you will.

All bitterness, anger and wrath, insult and slander must be removed from you, along with all wickedness. And be kind and compassionate to one another, forgiving one another, just as God also forgave you in Christ.

Ephesians 4:31-32 HCSB

Bitterness is a spiritual cancer, a rapidly growing malignancy that can consume your life. Bitterness cannot be ignored but must be healed at the very core, and only Christ can heal bitterness.

Beth Moore

By not forgiving, by not letting wrongs go, we aren't getting back at anyone. We are merely punishing ourselves by barricading our own hearts.

Jim Cymbala

He who cannot forgive others breaks the bridge over which he himself must pass.

Corrie ten Boom

You can never fully enjoy the present if you're bitter about the past. Instead of living in the past, make peace with it . . . and move on.

Day 11

Today's Big Question About Your Talents

Question:

God has given you special talents and unique opportunities. What should you do with your talents?

Answer:

Each person possesses special abilities that can be nurtured carefully or ignored totally. The challenge, of course, is to do the former and to avoid the latter.

Face it: you've got an array of talents that need to be refined—and you'll feel better about yourself when you refine them. But nobody will force you to do the hard work of converting raw talent into prime-time talent. That's a job you must do for yourself.

Today, make a promise to yourself that you will earnestly seek to discover the talents that God has given you. Then, nourish those talents and make them grow. Finally, vow to share your gifts with the world for as long as God gives you the power to do so. When you do, you'll feel better about yourself and your abilities . . . and the world will, too.

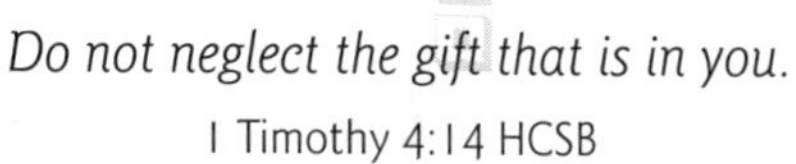
Do not neglect the gift that is in you.

1 Timothy 4:14 HCSB

You are the only person on earth who can use your ability.

Zig Ziglar

Employ whatever God has entrusted you with, in doing good, all possible good, in every possible kind and degree.

John Wesley

God often reveals His direction for our lives through the way He made us . . . with a certain personality and unique skills.

Bill Hybels

If you want to reach your potential, you need to add a strong work ethic to your talent.

John Maxwell

You have special abilities that can be nurtured carefully or ignored totally. The challenge, of course, is to do the former and to avoid the latter.

Day 12

Today's Big Question About Spiritual Growth

Question:

How important is it to keep growing spiritually?

Answer:

When it comes to your faith, God doesn't intend for you to stand still. He wants you to keep moving and growing. So promise yourself that your unfolding relationship with God will be your highest priority.

Are you about as mature as you're ever going to be? Hopefully not! When it comes to your faith, God doesn't intend for you to become "fully grown," at least not in this lifetime.

As a Christian, you should continue to grow in the love and the knowledge of your Savior as long as you live. How? By studying God's Word, by obeying His commandments, and by allowing His Son to reign over your heart.

Are you continually seeking to become a more mature believer? Hopefully so, because that's exactly what you owe to God and to yourself.

So let us stop going over the basics of Christianity again and again. Let us go on instead and become mature in our understanding.

Hebrews 6:1 NLT

A person who gazes and keeps on gazing at Jesus becomes like him in appearance.

E. Stanley Jones

The Scriptures were not given for our information, but for our transformation.

D. L. Moody

Approach the Scriptures not so much as a manual of Christian principles but as the testimony of God's friends on what it means to walk with him through a thousand different episodes.

John Eldredge

If you're determined to keep growing spiritually, you'll feel better about your world, your faith, and yourself. So keep growing . . . or else.

Day 13

Today's Big Question About Self-Respect

Question:

Perhaps you can be hard on yourself at times. What does the Bible say about your self-worth?

Answer:

You're made in God's image, and you're loved by Him. So you have great value, and you should think of yourself in that way.

What are you telling yourself about yourself? When you look in the mirror, are you staring back at your biggest booster or your harshest critic? If you can learn to give yourself the benefit of the doubt—if you can learn how to have constructive conversations with the person you see in the mirror—then your self-respect will tend to take care of itself. But, if you're constantly berating yourself—if you're constantly telling yourself that you can't measure up—then you'll find that self-respect is always in short supply.

Thoughts are intensely powerful things. Your thoughts have the power to lift you up or drag you down; they have the power to energize you or deplete you, to inspire you to greater accomplishments, or to make those accomplishments impossible.

The Bible teaches you to guard your thoughts against things that are hurtful or wrong (Proverbs 4:23). Yet sometimes you'll be tempted to let your thoughts run wild, especially if those thoughts are of the negative variety.

If you've acquired the habit of thinking constructively about yourself and your circumstances, congratulations. But if you're mired in the mental quicksand of overly self-critical thoughts, it's time to change your thoughts . . . and your life.

Give in to God, come to terms with him
and everything will turn out just fine.

Job 22:21 MSG

As you and I lay up for ourselves living, lasting treasures in Heaven, we come to the awesome conclusion that we ourselves are His treasure!

Anne Graham Lotz

Pay careful attention to the way that you evaluate yourself. And if you happen to be your own worst critic, it's time to reevaluate the way that you've been evaluating (got that?)

Day 14

Today's Big Question About Peer Pressure

Question:

Peer pressure is everywhere. What should you do?

Answer:

Face facts: Since you can't please everybody, you're better off trying to please God.

Who you are depends, to a surprising extent, on the people you hang out with. Peer pressure can be good or bad, depending upon who your peers are and how they behave. If your friends encourage you to follow God's will and to obey His commandments, then you'll experience positive peer pressure, and that's a good thing. But, if your friends encourage you to do foolish things, then you're facing a different kind of peer pressure . . . and you'd better beware.

Do you want to feel good about yourself and your life? If so, here's a simple, proven strategy: go out and find friends who, by their words and their actions, will help you build the kind of life that's worth feeling good about.

Whoever walks with the wise will become wise;
whoever walks with fools will suffer harm.

Proverbs 13:20 NLT

When we are set free from the bondage of pleasing others, when we are free from currying others' favor and others' approval—then no one will be able to make us miserable or dissatisfied. And then, if we know we have pleased God, contentment will be our consolation.

Kay Arthur

Nothing can be more dangerous than keeping wicked companions. They communicate the infection of their vices to all who associate with them.

St. Jean Baptiste de la Salle

Choose the opposition of the whole world rather than offend Jesus.

Thomas à Kempis

If you're hanging out with friends who behave badly, you're heading straight for trouble. To avoid negative consequences, pick friends who avoid negative behaviors.

Day 15

Today's Big Question About Mistakes

Question:

Mistakes happen. When they do, what should be done?

Answer:

If you've made a mistake, ask for forgiveness and start fixing what's broken! And if you've broken one of God's rules, you can always ask Him for His forgiveness. And He will always give it!

Everybody makes mistakes, and so will you. In fact, Winston Churchill once observed, "Success is going from failure to failure without loss of enthusiasm." What was good for Churchill is also good for you. You should expect to make mistakes—plenty of mistakes—but you should not allow those missteps to rob you of the enthusiasm you need to fulfill God's plan for your life.

We are imperfect people living in an imperfect world; mistakes are simply part of the price we pay for being here. But, even though mistakes are an inevitable part of life's journey, repeated mistakes should not be. When we commit the inevitable blunders of life, we must correct them, learn from them, and pray for the wisdom not to repeat them. When we do, our mistakes become lessons, and our lives become adventures in growth, not stagnation.

Have you made a mistake or three? Of course you have. But here's the big question: have you used your mistakes as stumbling blocks or stepping stones? The answer to that question will determine how well you will perform in every aspect of your life.

If you hide your sins, you will not succeed. If you confess and reject them, you will receive mercy.

Proverbs 28:13 NCV

Lord, when we are wrong, make us willing to change; and when we are right, make us easy to live with.

Peter Marshall

Very few things motivate us to give God our undivided attention like being faced with the negative consequences of our decisions.

Charles Stanley

Fix it sooner rather than later: When you make a mistake, the time to make things better is now, not later! The sooner you address your problem, the less stress you'll have to endure.

Day 16

Today's Big Question About The Need to Keep Learning

Question:

There's so much to learn. How can you keep up with it all?

Answer:

Simple: you've got to keep learning and growing every day of your life, not just when school is in session. And while you're at it, remember that real wisdom starts with God's Word, so be sure to start your day by reading the Bible every morning.

Another way to feel better about yourself is to keep acquiring both knowledge and wisdom. Knowledge is found in textbooks. Wisdom, on the other hand, is found in God's Holy Word and in the carefully-chosen words of loving parents, family members, and friends.

Knowledge is an important building block in a well-lived life, and it pays rich dividends both personally and professionally. But, wisdom is even more important because it refashions not only the mind, but also the heart.

When you study God's Word and live according to His commandments, you will become wise . . . and you will be a blessing to your family and to the world.

It takes knowledge to fill a home with rare and beautiful treasures.

Proverbs 24:4 NCV

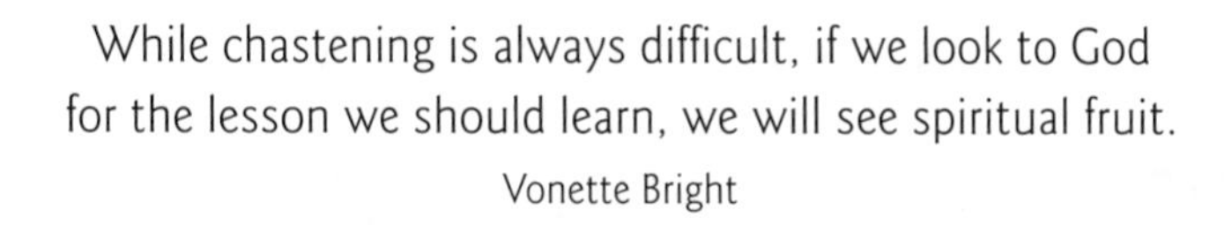

While chastening is always difficult, if we look to God for the lesson we should learn, we will see spiritual fruit.

Vonette Bright

The wonderful thing about God's schoolroom is that we get to grade our own papers. You see, He doesn't test us so He can learn how well we're doing. He tests us so we can discover how well we're doing.

Charles Swindoll

The wise man gives proper appreciation in his life to his past. He learns to sift the sawdust of heritage in order to find the nuggets that make the current moment have any meaning.

Grady Nutt

Keep learning. The future belongs to those who are willing to do the work that's required to prepare for it.

Day 17

Today's Big Question About Your Habits

Question:

If you've developed some bad habits, what should you do?

Answer:

Target your most unhealthy habit first, and attack it with vigor. When it comes to defeating harmful habitual behaviors, you'll need focus, determination, prayer, more focus, more determination, and more prayer.

It's an old saying and a true one: First, you make your habits, and then your habits make you. Some habits will inevitably bring you closer to God; other habits will lead you away from the path He has chosen for you. If you sincerely desire to improve your spiritual health, you must honestly examine the habits that make up the fabric of your day. And you must abandon those habits that are displeasing to God.

If you trust God, and if you keep asking for His help, He can transform your life. If you sincerely ask Him to help you, the same God who created the universe will help you defeat the harmful habits that have heretofore defeated you. So, if at first you don't succeed, keep praying. God is listening, and He's ready to help you become a better person if you ask Him . . . so ask today.

Abhor that which is evil; cleave to that which is good.

Romans 12:9 KJV

You can build up a set of good habits so that you habitually take the Christian way without thought.

E. Stanley Jones

You will never change your life until you change something you do daily.

John Maxwell

Since behaviors become habits, make them work with you and not against you.

E. Stanley Jones

If you want to form a new habit, get to work. If you want to break a bad habit, get on your knees.

Marie T. Freeman

First you make your habits; then your habits make you. So it's always a good time to think about the kind of person your habits are making you.

Day 18

Today's Big Question About God's Wisdom

Question:

What does the Bible say about the wisdom that can be found in God's Word?

Answer:

The Bible promises that God's wisdom is perfect. If you have questions, the Bible has the answers you need.

The world has its own brand of wisdom, a brand of wisdom that is often wrong and sometimes dangerous. God, on the other hand, has a different brand of wisdom, a wisdom that will lead you closer to Him.

Where will you place your trust today? Will you trust in the wisdom of fallible men and women, or will you place your faith God's perfect wisdom? The answer to this question will determine the direction of your day and the quality of your decisions.

Are you tired? Discouraged? Fearful? Be comforted and trust God. Are you worried or anxious? Be confident in God's power. Are you confused? Listen to the quiet voice of your Heavenly Father—He is not a God of confusion. Talk with Him; listen to Him; trust Him. His wisdom, unlike the "wisdom" of the world, will never let you down.

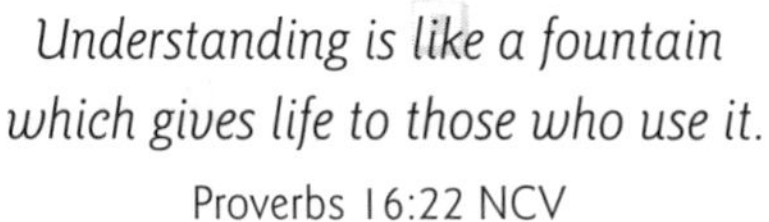

Understanding is like a fountain
which gives life to those who use it.
Proverbs 16:22 NCV

God does not give His counsel to the curious or the careless; He reveals His will to the concerned and to the consecrated.
Warren Wiersbe

Life isn't life without some divine decisions that our mortal minds simply cannot comprehend.
Beth Moore

The center of power is not to be found in summit meetings or in peace conferences. It is not in Peking or Washington or the United Nations, but rather where a child of God prays in the power of the Spirit for God's will to be done in her life, in her home, and in the world around her.
Ruth Bell Graham

God's wisdom is perfect, and it's available to you. So if you want to become wise, become a student of God's Word and a follower of His Son.

Day 19

Today's Big Question About God's Promises

Question:

The Bible makes many promises. Can you depend upon those promises?

Answer:

Yes! God is always faithful and His Word endures forever. So you and your family should study God's Word (every day) and trust it. When you do, you will be blessed.

God has made quite a few promises to you, and He intends to keep every single one of them. You will find these promises in a book like no other: the Holy Bible. The Bible is your roadmap for life here on earth and for life eternal—as a believer, you are called upon to trust its promises, to follow its commandments, and to share its Good News.

God has made promises to all of humanity and to you. God's promises never fail and they never grow old. You must trust those promises and share them with your family, with your friends, and with the world . . . starting now . . . and ending never.

God—His way is perfect; the word of the Lord is pure.
He is a shield to all who take refuge in Him.

Psalm 18:30 HCSB

The promises of Scripture are not mere pious hopes or sanctified guesses. They are more than sentimental words to be printed on decorated cards for Sunday School children. They are eternal verities. They are true. There is no perhaps about them.

Peter Marshall

God's promises are medicine for the broken heart. Let Him comfort you. And, after He has comforted you, try to share that comfort with somebody else. It will do both of you good.

Warren Wiersbe

Do you really trust God's promises, or are you hedging your bets? Today, think about the role that God's Word plays in your life, and think about ways that you can worry less and trust God more.

Day 20

Today's Big Question About Generosity

Question:

What does the Bible have to say about generosity?

Answer:

Generosity pays big dividends. So if you'd like to get more from life, try sharing more of the blessings that God has bestowed upon you. In other words, if you want to be happy, be generous. And if you want to be unhappy, be greedy.

Are you a cheerful giver? If you intend to obey God's commandments, you must be. When you give, God looks not only at the quality of your gift, but also at the condition of your heart. If you give generously, joyfully, and without complaint, you obey God's Word. But, if you make your gifts grudgingly, or if the motivation for your gift is selfish, you disobey your Creator, even if you have tithed in accordance with Biblical principles.

Today, take God's commandments to heart and make this pledge: Be a cheerful, generous, courageous giver. The world needs your help, and you need the spiritual rewards that will be yours when you give faithfully, prayerfully, and cheerfully.

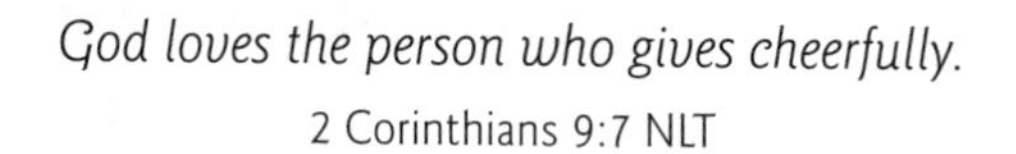

God loves the person who gives cheerfully.

2 Corinthians 9:7 NLT

Nothing is really ours until we share it.

C. S. Lewis

He climbs highest who helps another up.

Zig Ziglar

The mind grows by taking in,
but the heart grows by giving out.

Warren Wiersbe

We are never more like God than when we give.

Charles Swindoll

There is a direct relationship between generosity and joy—the more you give to others, the more joy you will experience for yourself.

Day 21

Today's Big Question About Finding Fulfillment

Question:

How can you find fulfillment?

Answer:

Fulfillment starts with God and ends there. If you honor God and welcome His Son into your heart, you'll find fulfillment, even when times are tough.

Where can we find contentment? Is it a result of wealth, power, or beauty, or fame? Hardly. Genuine contentment is a gift from God to those who trust Him and follow His commandments.

Our modern world seems preoccupied with the search for happiness. We are bombarded with messages telling us that happiness depends upon the acquisition of material possessions. These messages are false. Enduring peace is not the result of our acquisitions; it is a spiritual gift from God to those who obey Him and accept His will.

If we don't find contentment in God, we will never find it anywhere else. But, if we seek Him and obey Him, we will be blessed with an inner peace that is beyond human understanding. When God dwells at the center of our lives, peace and contentment will belong to us just as surely as we belong to God.

I am the Gate. Anyone who goes through me will be cared for—will freely go in and out, and find pasture. A thief is only there to steal and kill and destroy. I came so they can have real and eternal life, more and better life than they ever dreamed of. I am the Good Shepherd. The Good Shepherd puts the sheep before himself, sacrifices himself if necessary.

John 10:9-11 MSG

By trying to grab fulfillment everywhere, we find it nowhere.

Elisabeth Elliot

We will never be happy until we make God the source of our fulfillment and the answer to our longings.

Stormie Omartian

God's riches are beyond anything we could ask or even dare to imagine! If my life gets gooey and stale, I have no excuse.

Barbara Johnson

If you're not contented, try focusing less on "stuff" and more on God.

Day 22

Today's Big Question About Your Friends

Question:

What does the Bible say about my friends?

Answer:

Remember the first rule of friendship: it's the Golden one, and it starts like this: "Do unto others . . ." (Matthew 7:12).

When you hang out with positive people, you feel better about yourself and your world—when you hang out with negative people, you won't. So here's the question: do you want to feel better about yourself and your circumstances . . . or not? The answer you give should help you determine the friends you choose to make—and keep.

If you're really serious about being an optimistic, upbeat, hope-filled Christian, make sure that your friends feel the same way. Because if you choose to hang out with upbeat people, you'll tend to be an upbeat person, too. But if you hang out with the critics, the cynics, and the naysayers, you'll find yourself become a cynic, too. And life is far too short for that.

As iron sharpens iron, a friend sharpens a friend.

Proverbs 27:17 NLT

The next best thing to being wise oneself is to live in a circle of those who are.

C. S. Lewis

For better or worse, you will eventually become more and more like the people you associate with. So why not associate with people who make you better, not worse?

Marie T. Freeman

Yes, the Spirit was sent to be our Counselor. Yes, Jesus speaks to us personally. But often he works through another human being.

John Eldredge

Your friends will have a major impact on your self-image. That's an important reason (but not the only reason) to select your friends carefully.

Today's Big Question About Focusing On Jesus

Question:

What does God's Word say about God's Son?

Answer:

What a friend you have in Jesus: Jesus loves you, and He offers you eternal life with Him in heaven. Welcome Him into your heart. Now!

Is Christ the focus of your life? Are you fired with enthusiasm for Him? Are you an energized Christian who allows God's Son to reign over every aspect of your day? Make no mistake: that's exactly what God intends for you to do.

God has given you the gift of eternal life through His Son. In response to God's priceless gift, you are instructed to focus your thoughts, your prayers, and your energies upon God and His only begotten Son. To do so, you must resist the subtle yet powerful temptation to become a "spiritual dabbler."

A person who dabbles in the Christian faith is unwilling to place God in His rightful place: above all other things. Resist that temptation; make God the cornerstone and the touchstone of your life. When you do, He will give you all the strength and wisdom you need to live victoriously for Him.

For those whose lives are according to the flesh think about the things of the flesh, but those whose lives are according to the Spirit, about the things of the Spirit.

Romans 8:5 HCSB

Setting goals is one way you can be sure that you will focus your efforts on the main things so that trivial matters will not become your focus.

Charles Stanley

Forgetting your mission leads, inevitably, to getting tangled up in details—details that can take you completely off your path.

Laurie Beth Jones

Paul did one thing. Most of us dabble in forty things. Are you a doer or a dabbler?

Vance Havner

How much time do you spend focusing on God and His will for your life? If you answered, "Not much," it's time to reorder your priorities.

Day 24

Today's Big Question About Excuses

Question:

What does the Bible say about making excuses?

Answer:

God wants you to behave responsibly, and He doesn't want you to pass the buck. So instead of making excuses, do what needs to be done when it needs to be done.

Excuses are everywhere . . . excellence is not. Whether you're a student or even a corporate CEO, your work is a picture book of your priorities. So whatever your job description, it's up to you, and no one else, to become masterful at your craft. It's up to you to do your work right, and to do it right now.

Because we humans are such creative excuse-makers, all of the best excuses have already been taken—we've heard them all before.

So if you're wasting your time trying to concoct a new and improved excuse, don't bother. It's impossible. A far better strategy is this: do the work. Now. Then, let your excellent work speak loudly and convincingly for itself.

But each person should examine his own work,
and then he will have a reason for boasting in himself alone,
and not in respect to someone else.
For each person will have to carry his own load.
Galatians 6:4-5 HCSB

Replace your excuses with fresh determination.
Charles Swindoll

An excuse is only the skin of a reason stuffed with a lie.
Vance Havner

We need to stop focusing on our lacks and stop giving out excuses and start looking at and listening to Jesus.
Anne Graham Lotz

Today, think of something important that you've been putting off. Then think of the excuses you've used to avoid that responsibility. Finally, ask yourself what you can do today to finish the work you've been avoiding.

Day 25

Today's Big Question About Evil

Question:

This world can be a crazy place. What should you do about the evil that I encounter?

Answer:

Be careful and prayerful! There is darkness in this world, but God's light can overpower any darkness.

The better you get to know God, the more you'll understand how God wants you to respond to evil. And make no mistake, this world is inhabited by quite a few people who are very determined to do evil things. The devil and his human helpers are working 24/7 to cause pain and heartbreak in every corner of the globe . . . including your corner. So you'd better beware.

Your job, if you choose to accept it, is to recognize evil and fight it. The moment that you decide to fight evil whenever you see it, you can no longer be a lukewarm, halfhearted Christian. And, when you are no longer a lukewarm Christian, God rejoices while the devil despairs.

When will you choose to get serious about fighting the evils of our world? Before you answer that question, consider this: in the battle of good versus evil, the devil never takes a day off . . . and neither should you.

Take your stand with God's loyal community and live,
or chase after phantoms of evil and die.

Proverbs 11:19 MSG

God loves you, and He yearns for you to turn away from the path of evil. You need His forgiveness, and you need Him to come into your life and remake you from within.

Billy Graham

Rebuke the Enemy in your own name and he laughs; command him in the name of Christ and he flees.

John Eldredge

He who passively accepts evil is as much involved in it as he who helps to perpetrate it. He who accepts evil without protesting against it is really cooperating with it.

Martin Luther King, Jr.

Evil does exist, and you will confront it. Prepare yourself by forming a genuine, life-changing relationship with God and His only begotten Son. There is darkness in this world, but God's light can overpower any darkness.

Day 26

Today's Big Question About Envy

Question:

It's easy to envy other people. If you find yourself becoming envious, what should you do?

Answer:

Remember this: You can be envious, or you can be happy, but you can't be both. Envy and happiness can't live at the same time in the same brain.

Because we are frail, imperfect human beings, we are sometimes envious of others. But God's Word warns us that envy is sin. Thus, we must guard ourselves against the natural tendency to feel resentment and jealousy when other people experience good fortune. As believers, we have absolutely no reason to be envious of any people on earth. After all, as Christians we are already recipients of the greatest gift in all creation: God's grace. We have been promised the gift of eternal life through God's only begotten Son, and we must count that gift as our most precious possession.

So here's a simple suggestion that is guaranteed to bring you happiness: fill your heart with God's love, God's promises, and God's Son . . . and when you do so, leave no room for envy, hatred, bitterness, or regret.

Therefore, laying aside all malice, all deceit, hypocrisy, envy, and all evil speaking, as newborn babes, desire the pure milk of the word, that you may grow thereby.

I Peter 2:1-2 NKJV

How can you possess the miseries of envy when you possess in Christ the best of all portions?

C. H. Spurgeon

Is there somebody who's always getting your goat? Talk to the Shepherd.

Anonymous

What God asks, does, or requires of others is not my business; it is His.

Kay Arthur

Envy is a sin, a sin that robs you of contentment and peace. So you must steadfastly refuse to let feelings of envy invade your thoughts or your heart.

Day 27

Today's Big Question About Drugs

Question:

Drugs are everywhere. What should you do?

Answer:

Drugs are addictive, dangerous, destructive, and potentially deadly. Avoid them. And while you're at it, avoid the people who use them.

Do you hang out with people who consider "partying" to be the most important aspect of their lives? If so, you're headed headlong down a dead-end street . . . right along with your friends.

Mind-altering substances (including the most popular American mind-bender of all: beer) are dangerous . . . make that Dangerous (with a capital D).

So here are three things to remember about alcohol and other drugs: 1. If you're drinking or drugging, you must either stop that behavior or face very disastrous consequences. 2. If you're spending time with people who think that alcohol and drugs are "harmless," you're choosing to associate with some very naïve people. 3. If you're dating someone who drinks or does drugs, you deserve better . . . much better. End of lecture.

Be sober! Be on the alert! Your adversary the Devil is prowling around like a roaring lion, looking for anyone he can devour.

I Peter 5:8 HCSB

One reason I'm a teetotaler is that I got so disgusted being mistreated due to a man's drinking to excess that I never have wanted to run the risk of mistreating my own family by drinking.

Jerry Clower

Addiction is the most powerful psychic enemy of humanity's desire for God.

Gerald May

Whatever you love most, be it sports, pleasure, business or God, that is your god.

Billy Graham

Make Jesus your highest priority, and ask Him to help you overcome any behaviors that might distance you from Him.

Day 28

Today's Big Question About Character

Question:

You hear lots of people talking about character. But is it really that important?

Answer:

Remember: Character is more important than popularity.

Beth Moore correctly observed, "Those who walk in truth walk in liberty." Godly guys and girls agree. As believers in Christ, we must seek to live each day with discipline, honesty, and faith. When we do, at least two things happen: integrity becomes a habit, and God blesses us because of our obedience to Him. Living a life of integrity isn't always the easiest way, but in the long run, it's the more peaceful—and less stressful—way to live.

Character isn't built overnight; it is built slowly over a lifetime. It is the sum of every sensible choice, every honorable decision, and every honest word. It is forged on the anvil of sincerity and polished by the virtue of fairness. Character is a precious thing—preserve yours at all costs.

In all things showing yourself to be a pattern of good works; in doctrine showing integrity, reverence, incorruptibility . . . .

Titus 2:7 NKJV

Image is what people think we are;
integrity is what we really are.

John Maxwell

Integrity is the glue that holds our way of life together. We must constantly strive to keep our integrity intact. When wealth is lost, nothing is lost; when health is lost, something is lost; when character is lost, all is lost.

Billy Graham

The man who cannot believe in himself cannot believe in anything else. The basis of all integrity and character is whatever faith we have in our own integrity.

Roy L. Smith

When your words are honest and your intentions are pure, you have nothing to fear. Thus, you should guard your integrity even more carefully than you guard your wallet.

Day 29

Today's Big Question About Cheerfulness

Question:

Why is it important for you to have a cheerful disposition?

Answer:

As a Christian, you have more blessings than you can count, which means you've got lots to be cheerful about. And remember: cheerfulness, like its opposite, is contagious. So cheer up!

Few things in life are more sad, or, for that matter, more absurd, than a grumpy Christian. Christ promises us lives of abundance and joy, but He does not force His joy upon us. We must claim His joy for ourselves, and when we do, Jesus, in turn, fills our spirits with His power and His love.

How can we receive from Christ the joy that is rightfully ours? By giving Him what is rightfully His: our hearts and our souls.

When we earnestly commit ourselves to the Savior of mankind, when we place Jesus at the center of our lives and trust Him as our personal Savior, He will transform us, not just for today, but for all eternity. Then we, as God's children, can share Christ's joy and His message with a world that needs both.

A cheerful heart has a continual feast.

Proverbs 15:15 HCSB

Christ can put a spring in your step and
a thrill in your heart. Optimism and cheerfulness are
products of knowing Christ.

Billy Graham

Be assured, my dear friend, that it is no joy to God
in seeing you with a dreary countenance.

C. H. Spurgeon

The people whom I have seen succeed best in life have always
been cheerful and hopeful people who went about their
business with a smile on their faces.

Charles Kingsley

Do you need a little cheering up? If so, find somebody else who needs cheering up, too. Then, do your best to brighten that person's day. When you do, you'll discover that cheering up other people is a wonderful way to cheer yourself up, too!

Day 30

Today's Big Question About Celebrating Life

Question:

Why should you be excited about life?

Answer:

When you stop long enough to think (and to pray) about it, you'll realize that today, and every day, is a cause for celebration. So plan your day—and your life—accordingly.

Are you living the triumphant life that God has promised? Or are you, instead, a spiritual shrinking violet? As you ponder that question, consider this: God does not intend that you live a life that is commonplace or mediocre. And He doesn't want you to hide your light "under a basket." Instead, He wants you to "Let your light so shine before men, that they may see your good works and glorify your Father in heaven" (Matthew 5:16 NKJV). In short, God wants you to live a triumphant life so that others might know precisely what it means to be a believer.

The Christian life should be a triumphal celebration, a daily exercise in thanksgiving and praise. Join that celebration today. And while you're at it, make sure that you let everybody—friends, family members, and dates—know that you've joined.

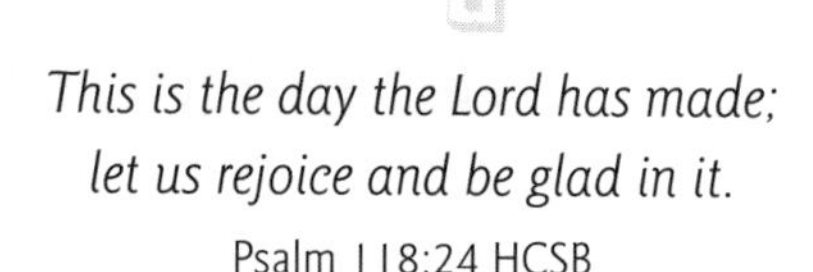

This is the day the Lord has made;
let us rejoice and be glad in it.

Psalm 118:24 HCSB

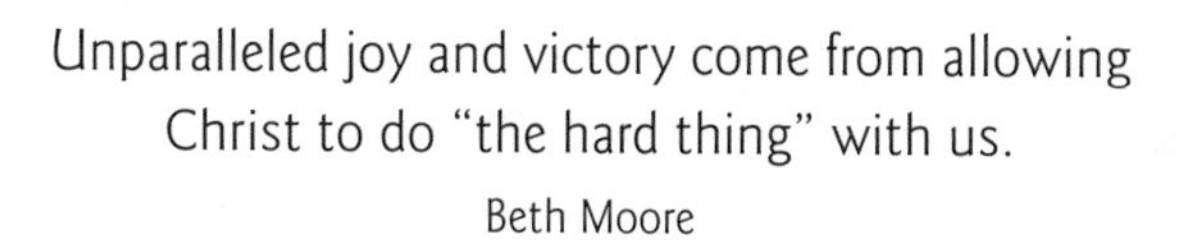

Unparalleled joy and victory come from allowing Christ to do "the hard thing" with us.

Beth Moore

Some of us seem so anxious about avoiding hell that we forget to celebrate our journey toward heaven.

Philip Yancey

If you can forgive the person you were, accept the person you are, and believe in the person you will become, you are headed for joy. So celebrate your life.

Barbara Johnson

Don't overlook God's gifts. Every sunrise represents yet another beautifully wrapped gift from God. Unwrap it; treasure it; use it; and give thanks to the Giver.

Day 31

Today's Big Question About Your Thoughts

Question:

How does the Bible instruct me to direct my thoughts?

Answer:

You must watch what you think because your attitude is important. If your inner voice is, in reality, your inner critic, you need to tone down the criticism now. And while you're at it, train yourself to begin thinking thoughts that are more rational, more accepting, and less judgmental.

How will you direct your thoughts today? Will you obey the words of Philippians 4:8 by dwelling upon those things that are honorable, just, and commendable? Or will you allow your thoughts to be hijacked by the negativity that seems to dominate our troubled world? Are you fearful, angry, stressed, or worried? Are you so preoccupied with the concerns of this day that you fail to thank God for the promise of eternity? Are you confused, bitter, or pessimistic? If so, God wants to have a little talk with you.

God intends that you experience joy and abundance. So, today and every day hereafter, celebrate the life that God has given you by focusing your thoughts upon those things that are worthy of praise. Today, count your blessings instead of your hardships. And thank the Giver of all things good for gifts that are simply too numerous to count.

Finally brothers, whatever is true, whatever is honorable, whatever is just, whatever is pure, whatever is lovely, whatever is commendable—if there is any moral excellence and if there is any praise—dwell on these things.

Philippians 4:8 HCSB

I may not be able to change the world I see around me, but I can change the way I see the world within me.

John Maxwell

The mind is like a clock that is constantly running down. It has to be wound up daily with good thoughts.

Fulton J. Sheen

Today, create a positive attitude by focusing on opportunities, not roadblocks. Of course you may have experienced disappointments in the past, and you will undoubtedly experience some setbacks in the future. But don't invest large amounts of energy focusing on past misfortunes. Instead, look to the future with optimism and hope.

Today's Big Question About Your Behavior

Question:

How does God want you and your friends to behave?

Answer:

If you're not sure that it's the right thing to do, don't do it! And if you're not sure that it's the truth, don't tell it.

It's simple: If you want to hold things together, you must obey God. But obeying Him isn't always easy. You live in a world that presents countless temptations to stray far from God's path. So here's some timely advice: when you're confronted with sin, walk—or better yet run—in the opposite direction.

When you seek righteousness for yourself—and when we seek the companionship of people who do likewise—you will reap the spiritual rewards that God has in store for you. When you live in accordance with God's commandments, you will be blessed. When you genuinely seek to follow in the footsteps of God's Son, you will experience God's presence, God's peace, and God's abundance.

So make yourself this promise: Support only those activities that further God's kingdom and your own spiritual growth. Then, prepare to reap the blessings that God has promised to all those who live according to His will and His Word.

Knowing what is right is like deep water in the heart;
a wise person draws from the well within.

Proverbs 20:5 MSG

Either God's Word keeps you from sin,
or sin keeps you from God's Word.

Corrie ten Boom

Many people never receive God's best for them
because they are addicted to the approval of others.

Joyce Meyer

What you do reveals what you believe about God,
regardless of what you say. When God reveals what He has
purposed to do, you face a crisis—a decision time.
God and the world can tell from your response what you
really believe about God.

Henry Blackaby

When it comes to doing the right thing, don't put it off. If you're not willing to do the right thing today, why should you (or anybody else, for that matter) expect you to change tomorrow?

Day 33

Today's Big Question About Abstinence

Question:

Okay, the world glorifies sex; the world even promotes it. But what does God want for me to do?

Answer:

The world often seems to glorify premarital sex. God does not. Trust God.

The decision to have sex before you're married—or the decision to abstain from it—is a choice that will most certainly impact the rest of your life. That decision will play an important role in the way you see yourself, and it will play an important role in the way you view relationships with members of the opposite sex. And of course, there's always the chance that your decision to have sex might result in an unexpected "surprise."

Face it: there's a lot riding on the decision to abstain from sex. And because it's an important decision, you should think about it—and pray about it—before you make a decision that might just change the direction of your life.

As you're making up your mind about the role that sex will play in your life, trust the quiet inner voice of your conscience, and be obedient to the teaching you find in God's Word.

Therefore, brothers, by the mercies of God, I urge you to present your bodies as a living sacrifice, holy and pleasing to God; this is your spiritual worship.

Romans 12:1 HCSB

A pure theology and a loose morality will never mix.

C. H. Spurgeon

A life lived in God is not lived on the plane of feelings, but of the will.

Elisabeth Elliot

Morality and immorality are not defined by man's changing attitudes and social customs. They are determined by the God of the universe, whose timeless standards cannot be ignored with impunity.

James Dobson

If you are a Christian, your hero (and the One you should seek to imitate) is Christ. So follow in His footsteps and obey His commandments. When you do, you'll be secure.

Day 34

Today's Big Question About Kindness

Question:

Sometimes it's so easy to overlook the needs of others. What does the Bible instruct me to do?

Answer:

You can't just talk about it: In order to be a kind person, you must not only think kind thoughts, you must also do kind things. So get busy! The time to be kind is now.

Kindness is a choice. Sometimes, when we feel happy or generous, we find it easy to be kind. Other times, when we are discouraged or tired, we can scarcely summon the energy to utter a single kind word. But, God's commandment is clear: He intends that we make the conscious choice to treat others with kindness and respect, no matter our circumstances, no matter our emotions.

In the busyness and confusion of daily life, it is easy to lose focus, and it is easy to become frustrated. We are imperfect human beings struggling to manage our lives as best we can, but we often fall short. When we are distracted or disappointed, we may neglect to share a kind word or a kind deed. This oversight hurts others, but it hurts us most of all.

Today, slow yourself down and be alert for people who need your smile, your kind words, or your helping hand. Make kindness a centerpiece of your dealings with others. They will be blessed, and you will be too.

And be kind and compassionate to one another, forgiving one another, just as God also forgave you in Christ.

Ephesians 4:32 HCSB

When you extend hospitality to others,
you're not trying to impress people,
you're trying to reflect God to them.

Max Lucado

When you launch an act of kindness out into
the crosswinds of life, it will blow kindness back to you.

Dennis Swanberg

The Golden Rule starts with you, so when in doubt, be a little kinder than necessary. You'll feel better about yourself when you do.

Day 35

Today's Big Question About Your Choices

Question:

You make lots of choices every day. How does God want you to choose?

Answer:

You choices are important. First you'll make choices, and before you know it, your choices will make you. So God wants you to choose carefully.

Your life is a series of choices. From the instant you wake up in the morning until the moment you nod off to sleep at night, you make countless decisions—decisions about the things you do, decisions about the words you speak, and decisions about the way that you choose to direct your thoughts.

As a believer who has been transformed by the love of Jesus, you have every reason to make wise choices. But sometimes, when the stresses of the daily grind threaten to grind you up and spit you out, you may make choices that are displeasing to God. When you do, you'll pay a price because you'll forfeit the happiness and the peace that might otherwise have been yours.

So, as you pause to consider the kind of Christian you are—and the kind of Christian you want to become—ask yourself whether you're sitting on the fence or standing in the light. The choice is yours . . . and so are the consequences.

But the wisdom from above is first pure, then peace-loving, gentle, compliant, full of mercy and good fruits, without favoritism and hypocrisy.

James 3:17 HCSB

The greatest choice any man makes is to let God choose for him.

Vance Havner

Every step of your life's journey is a choice . . . and the quality of those choices determines the quality of the journey.

Criswell Freeman

Little decisions, when made over a long period of time, can have big consequences. So remember that when it comes to matters of health, fitness, stress, and spirituality, there are no small decisions.

Day 36

Today's Big Question About Going to Church

Question:

It's tempting to skip church. Is it really all that important for you to attend church regularly?

Answer:

You need church more than the church needs you. What you put into church determines what you get out of it. So think of church as a celebration, not an obligation.

If you're falling apart, there's a place you can go to put yourself back together. It's a place spelled c-h-u-r-c-h.

In the Book of Acts, Luke reminds us to "feed the church of God" (20:28). As Christians who have been saved by a loving, compassionate Creator, we are compelled not only to worship Him in our hearts but also to worship Him in the presence of fellow believers.

Do you attend church regularly? And when you attend, are you an active participant, or are you just taking up space? The answer to these questions will have a profound impact on the quality and direction of your spiritual journey.

So do yourself a favor: become actively involved in your church. Don't just go to church out of habit. Go to church out of a sincere desire to know and worship God.

The church, you see, is not peripheral to the world;
the world is peripheral to the church.
The church is Christ's body, in which he speaks and acts,
by which he fills everything with his presence.

Ephesians 1:23 MSG

To model the kingdom of God in the world,
the church must not only be a repentant community,
committed to truth, but also a holy community.

Chuck Colson

The Bible knows nothing of solitary religion.

John Wesley

It has always been the work of the church
to bring others to belief in Christ and to experience
a personal relationship with Him.

Charles Stanley

Make church a celebration, not an obligation: Your attitude towards church is important, in part, because it is contagious . . . so celebrate accordingly!

Day 37

Today's Big Question About Distractions

Question:

The world seems filled with distractions. How can you focus more intently on the things that really matter?

Answer:

Have a daily devotional every morning, keep praying throughout the day, and don't support any activity that distances you from God's path or from your most important priorities. Put first things first, starting with God.

All of us must live through those days when the traffic jams, the computer crashes, and the dog makes a main course out of our homework. But, when we find ourselves distracted by the minor frustrations of life, we must catch ourselves, take a deep breath, and lift our thoughts upward.

Although we may, at times, struggle mightily to rise above the distractions of everyday living, we need never struggle alone. God is here—eternal and faithful, with infinite patience and love—and, if we reach out to Him, He will restore our sense of perspective and give peace to our souls.

Look straight ahead, and fix your eyes on what lies before you.
Mark out a straight path for your feet;
then stick to the path and stay safe. Don't get sidetracked;
keep your feet from following evil.

Proverbs 4:25-27 NLT

We need to stop focusing on our lacks and stop giving out excuses and start looking at and listening to Jesus.

Anne Graham Lotz

Paul did one thing. Most of us dabble in forty things. Are you a doer or a dabbler?

Vance Havner

When Jesus is in our midst, He brings His limitless power along as well. But, Jesus must be in the middle, all eyes and hearts focused on Him.

Shirley Dobson

With all the distractions in the world, let Jesus be your main attraction.

Today's Big Question About Decisions

Question:
Making big decisions can be hard. What should you do?

Answer:
Before you make any big decision, you should think carefully, pray earnestly, talk to people you trust, and listen carefully to your conscience.

Life presents each of us with countless questions, conundrums, doubts, and problems. Thankfully, the riddles of everyday living are not too difficult to solve if we look for answers in the right places. When we have questions, we should consult God's Word, we should consult our own consciences, and we should consult a few close friends and family members.

Perhaps Søren Kierkegaard was stating the obvious when he observed, "Life can only be understood backwards; but it must be lived forwards." Still, Kierkegaard's words are far easier to understand than they are to live by.

Taking a forward-looking (and stress-conquering) approach to life means learning the art of solving difficult problems sensibly and consistently . . . and sooner rather than later.

If you need wisdom—if you want to know what God wants you to do—ask him, and he will gladly tell you. He will not resent your asking.

James 1:5 NLT

Successful people make right decisions early and manage those decisions daily.

John Maxwell

No trumpets sound when the important decisions of our life are made. Destiny is made known silently.

Agnes DeMille

Life is built on character, but character is built on decisions.

Warren Wiersbe

Never take on a major obligation of any kind without first taking sufficient time to carefully consider whether or not you should commit to it. The bigger the obligation, the more days you should take to decide. If someone presses you for an answer before you are ready, your automatic answer should always be "No."

Day 39

Today's Big Question About Getting Things Done

Question:

Sometimes, you know the thing that needs to be done, but taking action is hard. What should you do?

Answer:

Pray as if everything depended upon God, and work as if everything depended on you.

It's true: actions do speak louder than words. And as believers, we must beware: our actions should always give credence to the changes that Christ can make in the lives of those who walk with Him.

God calls upon each of us to act in accordance with His will and with respect for His commandments. If we are to be responsible believers, we must realize that it is never enough simply to hear the instructions of God; we must also live by them. And it is never enough to wait idly by while others do God's work here on earth; we, too, must act. Doing God's work is a responsibility that each of us must bear, and when we do, our loving Heavenly Father rewards our efforts with a bountiful harvest.

For the kingdom of God is not in talk but in power.

I Corinthians 4:20 HCSB

Do noble things, do not dream them all day long.

Charles Kingsley

Every word we speak, every action we take,
has an effect on the totality of humanity.
No one can escape that privilege—or that responsibility.

Laurie Beth Jones

Never fail to do something because you don't feel like it.
Sometimes you just have to do it now,
and you'll feel like it later.

Marie T. Freeman

Try as we might, we simply cannot escape the consequences of our actions. How we behave today has a direct impact on the rewards we will receive tomorrow. That's a lesson that we must teach our students by our words and our actions, but not necessarily in that order.

Day 40

Today's Big Question About God's Protection

Question:

What does the Bible say about God's role in your life?

Answer:

The Bible promises that you are protected by God . . . now and always. Earthly security is an illusion. Your only real security comes from the loving heart of God.

It's a promise that is made over and over again in the Bible: Whatever "it" is, God can handle it.

Life isn't always easy. Far from it! Sometimes, life can be very, very difficult, indeed. But even when the storm clouds form overhead, even during our most stressful moments, we're protected by a loving Heavenly Father.

When we're worried, God can reassure us; when we're sad, God can comfort us. When our hearts are broken, God is not just near; He is here. So we must lift our thoughts and prayers to Him. When we do, He will answer our prayers. Why? Because He is our Shepherd, and He has promised to protect us now and forever.

I will lift up my eyes to the hills. From whence comes my help? My help comes from the Lord, Who made heaven and earth.

Psalm 121:1-2 NKJV

God is God whether we recognize it or not. Nothing about that can change, except us.

Lisa Whelchel

Either we are adrift in chaos or we are individuals, created, loved, upheld and placed purposefully, exactly where we are. Can you believe that? Can you trust God for that?

Elisabeth Elliot

God is in control, and therefore in everything I can give thanks, not because of the situation, but because of the One who directs and rules over it.

Kay Arthur

Remember that God can handle your problems. Bill Hybels writes, "Pour out your heart to God and tell Him how you feel. Be real, be honest, and when you get it all out, you'll start to feel the gradual covering of God's comforting presence." Enough said.

Day 41

Today's Big Question About Your Gifts

Question:

You have talents and opportunities that are uniquely yours. What does the Bible say about that?

Answer:

God has given you many gifts, and He intends for you to use them. If you use your gifts wisely, they're multiplied. If you misuse your gifts—or ignore them altogether—they are lost.

How do we thank God for the gifts He has given us? By using those gifts, that's how!

God has given you talents and opportunities that are uniquely yours. Are you willing to use your gifts in the way that God intends? And are you willing to summon the discipline that is required to develop your talents and to hone your skills? That's precisely what God wants you to do, and that's precisely what you should desire for yourself.

As you seek to expand your talents, you will undoubtedly encounter stumbling blocks along the way, such as the fear of rejection or the fear of failure. When you do, don't stumble! Just continue to refine your skills, and offer your services to God. And when the time is right, He will use you—but it's up to you to be thoroughly prepared when He does.

I remind you to keep ablaze the gift of God that is in you.

2 Timothy 1:6 HCSB

God has given you special talents—
now it's your turn to give them back to God.

Marie T. Freeman

You are the only person on earth
who can use your ability.

Zig Ziglar

The Lord has abundantly blessed me all of my life.
I'm not trying to pay Him back for all of His wonderful gifts;
I just realize that He gave them to me to give away.

Lisa Whelchel

God has given you a unique array of talents and opportunities. If you use your gifts wisely, they're multiplied. If you misuse your gifts—or ignore them altogether—they are lost. God is anxious for you to use your gifts . . . are you?

Day 42

Today's Big Question About God's Guidance

Question:

If you want God to guide you, what should you do?

Answer:

If you want God's guidance, ask for it. When you pray for guidance, God will give it.

The Bible promises that God will guide you if you let Him. Your job is to let Him. But sometimes, you will be tempted to do otherwise. Sometimes, you'll be tempted to go along with the crowd; other times, you'll be tempted to do things your way, not God's way. When you feel these temptations, resist them.

God has promised that when you ask for His help, He will not withhold it. So ask. Ask Him to meet the needs of your day. Ask Him to lead you, to protect you, and to correct you. And trust the answers He gives.

God stands at the door and waits. When you knock, He opens. When you ask, He answers. Your task, of course, is to seek His guidance prayerfully, confidently, and often.

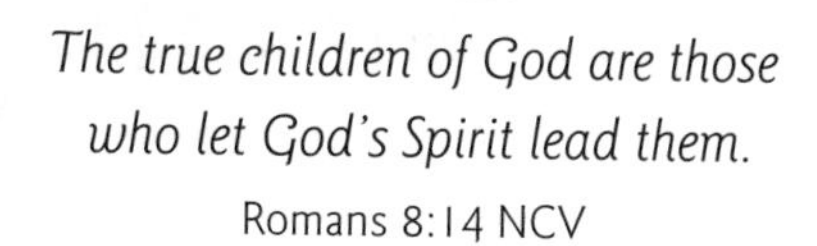

The true children of God are those
who let God's Spirit lead them.

Romans 8:14 NCV

If we want to hear God's voice,
we must surrender our minds and hearts to Him.

Billy Graham

We have ample evidence that the Lord is able to guide.
The promises cover every imaginable situation.
All we need to do is to take the hand he stretches out.

Elisabeth Elliot

Only He can guide you to invest your life in worthwhile ways. This guidance will come as you "walk" with Him and listen to Him.

Henry Blackaby and Claude King

Is God your spare wheel or your steering wheel? Would you like God's guidance? Then ask Him for it. When you pray for guidance, God will give it (Luke 11:9). So ask.

Today's Big Question About God's Love

Question:

What does the Bible say about God's love?

Answer:

When all else fails, God's love does not. You can always depend upon God's love . . . and He is always your ultimate protection.

God loves you. How will you respond to His love? The Bible clearly defines what your response should be: "You shall love the Lord your God with all your heart, with all your soul, and with all your strength" (Deuteronomy 6:5 NKJV). But you must not stop there. You must also love your neighbor as yourself. Jesus teaches that "On these two commandments hang all the Law and the Prophets" (Matthew 22:40).

Today, as you meet the demands of everyday living, will you pause long enough to return God's love? And then will you share it? Prayerfully, you will. When you embrace God's love, you are forever changed. When you embrace God's love, you feel differently about yourself, your family, your friends, and your world. When you embrace God's love, you have enough love to keep and enough love to share: enough love for a day, enough love for a lifetime, enough love for all eternity.

My dear, dear friends, if God loved us like this,
we certainly ought to love each other.

1 John 4:11 MSG

When you agree to let God love the unlovely through you,
He never fails to make the unlovely lovely to you.

Beth Moore

Although our actions have nothing to do with gaining our own salvation, they might be used by God to save somebody else! What we do really matters, and it can affect the eternities of people we care about.

Bill Hybels

As I spent time with God, growing in my knowledge of Him through prayer, Bible Study, obedience, and submission, He would fill my life. And because God is love and because He would fill me, His love would fill me.

Anne Graham Lotz

Be creative: There are many ways to say, "I love you." Find them. Use them. And keep using them.

Day 44

Today's Big Question About Gossip

Question:

What does God's Word say about gossip?

Answer:

The Bible warns against gossip. So don't do it!

Face facts: gossip is the guilty little pleasure that tempts almost all of us from time to time. Why is it so tempting to gossip? Because when we put other people down, we experience a brief dose of self-righteousness as we look down our noses at the misdeeds of others. But there's a catch: in truth, we can never really build ourselves up by tearing other people down. So the habit of gossip turns out to be a self-defeating waste of time.

It's no wonder that the Bible clearly teaches that gossip is wrong. Consider the simple advice found in Proverbs 16:28: "Gossip ruins friendships" (NCV). So do yourself a big favor: don't spend precious time talking about other people. It's a waste of words, it's the wrong thing to do, and in the end, it will leave you with less self-respect, not more.

When you avoid the temptation to engage in gossip, you'll feel better about yourself—and other people will feel better about you, too. So don't do it.

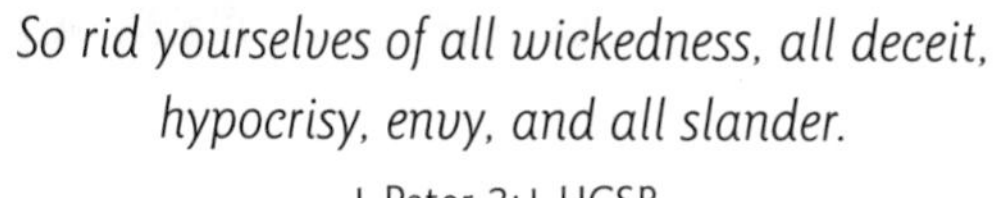

So rid yourselves of all wickedness, all deceit, hypocrisy, envy, and all slander.

I Peter 2:1 HCSB

The cost of gossip always exceeds its worth.

Marie T. Freeman

Change the heart, and you change the speech.

Warren Wiersbe

The great test of a man's character is his tongue.

Oswald Chambers

To belittle is to be little.

Anonymous

When talking about other people, use this guideline: don't say something behind someone's back that you wouldn't say to that person directly.

Day 45

Today's Big Question About Hope

Question:

Sometimes it's hard to be hopeful. What does the Bible say about hope?

Answer:

Don't give up hope: Other people have experienced the same kind of hard times you may be experiencing now. They made it, and so can you.

There are few sadder sights on earth than the sight of a girl or guy who has lost hope. In difficult times, hope can be elusive, but those who place their faith in God's promises need never lose it. After all, God is good; His love endures; He has promised His children the gift of eternal life. And, God keeps His promises.

If you find yourself falling into the spiritual traps of worry and discouragement, seek the healing touch of Jesus and the encouraging words of fellow believers. And if you find a friend in need, remind him or her of the peace that is found through a genuine relationship with Christ. It was Christ who promised, "I have told you these things so that in Me you may have peace. In the world you have suffering. But take courage! I have conquered the world" (John 16:33 HCSB). This world can be a place of trials and troubles, but as believers, we are secure. God has promised us peace, joy, and eternal life. And, of course, God keeps His promises today, tomorrow, and forever.

You, Lord, give true peace to those who depend on you, because they trust you.

Isaiah 26:3 NCV

Hope is faith holding out its hand in the dark.

Barbara Johnson

The will of God is the most delicious and delightful thing in the universe.

Hannah Whitall Smith

It is more serious to lose hope than to sin.

John of Carpathos

If you're experiencing hard times, you'll be wise to start spending more time with God. And if you do your part, God will do His part. So never be afraid to hope—or to ask—for a miracle.

Day 46

Today's Big Question About Impulsivity

Question:

Sometimes it's easy to act first and think second. What does the Bible say about that?

Answer:

The Bible warns against impulsive behavior. So before you do something you might regret, slow down and think things through.

Maybe you've heard this old saying: "Look before you leap." Well, that saying may be old, but it still applies to you. Before you jump into something, you should look ahead and plan ahead. Otherwise, you might soon be sorry you jumped!

When you acquire the habit of thinking ahead and planning ahead, you'll make better choices (and, as a result, you'll feel better about yourself).

So when it comes to the important things in life, don't allow impulsive behavior to dynamite your future. Think long and hard about the consequences of your actions before you do something foolish . . . or dangerous . . . or both.

I will instruct you and teach you in the way you should go;
I will guide you with My eye.

Psalm 32:8 NKJV

Sometimes, being wise is nothing more than slowing down long enough to think about things before you do them.

Marie T. Freeman

It's incredible to realize that what we do each day has meaning in the big picture of God's plan.

Bill Hybels

Allow your dreams a place in your prayers and plans. God-given dreams can help you move into the future He is preparing for you.

Barbara Johnson

Think ahead—it's the best way of making sure you don't get left behind.

Day 47

Today's Big Question About Judging Other People

Question:

It's hard not to be judgmental of other people, and it's hard not to judge their motives. What does the Bible say about judging others?

Answer:

Your ability to judge others requires a divine insight that you simply don't have. So do everybody (including yourself) a favor: don't judge.

Here's something worth thinking about: If you judge other people harshly, God will judge you in the same fashion. But that's not all (thank goodness!). The Bible also promises that if you forgive others, you, too, will be forgiven. Have you developed the bad habit of behaving yourself like an amateur judge and jury, assigning blame and condemnation wherever you go? If so, it's time to grow up and obey God.

When it comes to judging everything and everybody, God doesn't need your help . . . and He doesn't want it. So the next time you're beset by the temptation to judge another human being's motives, catch yourself before you make that mistake. Don't be a judge; be a witness.

Stop judging others, and you will not be judged.
Stop criticizing others, or it will all come back on you.
If you forgive others, you will be forgiven.

Luke 6:37 NLT

Christians think they are prosecuting attorneys or judges, when, in reality, God has called all of us to be witnesses.

Warren Wiersbe

Don't judge other people more harshly than you want God to judge you.

Marie T. Freeman

Turn your attention upon yourself and beware of judging the deeds of other men, for in judging others a man labors vainly, often makes mistakes, and easily sins; whereas, in judging and taking stock of himself he does something that is always profitable.

Thomas à Kempis

To the extent you judge others, so, too, will you be judged. So you must, to the best of your ability, refrain from judgmental thoughts and words.

Day 48

Today's Big Question About Listening to God

Question:

What does the Bible say about listening to God?

Answer:

If you and your family members want to gain a more intimate relationship with God, you should study His Word (every day), worship Him (every day), and talk to Him (many times every day). Remember: The more often you speak to the Creator, the more often He'll speak to you.

Sometimes God speaks loudly and clearly. More often, He speaks in a quiet voice—and if you are wise, you will be listening carefully when He does. To do so, you must carve out quiet moments each day to study His Word and sense His direction.

Can you quiet yourself long enough to listen to your conscience? Are you attuned to the subtle guidance of your intuition? Are you willing to pray sincerely and then to wait quietly for God's response? Hopefully so. Usually God refrains from sending His messages on stone tablets or city billboards. More often, He communicates in subtler ways. If you sincerely desire to hear His voice, you must listen carefully, and you must do so in the silent corners of your quiet, willing heart.

The one who is from God listens to God's words.
This is why you don't listen, because you are not from God.
John 8:47 HCSB

In the soul-searching of our lives,
we are to stay quiet so we can hear Him say
all that He wants to say to us in our hearts.
Charles Swindoll

When we come to Jesus stripped of pretensions,
with a needy spirit, ready to listen,
He meets us at the point of need.
Catherine Marshall

God is always listening.
Stormie Omartian

Listening is loving.
Zig Ziglar

Prayer is two-way communication with God. Talking to God isn't enough; you should also listen to Him.

Day 49

Today's Big Question About Guarding Your Heart

Question:

The world is a difficult and dangerous place What should you do?

Answer:

God's Word warns you to be on guard against evil and to guard your heart.

You are near and dear to God. He loves you more than you can imagine, and He wants the very best for you. And one more thing: God wants you to guard your heart.

Every day, you are faced with choices . . . lots of them. You can do the right thing, or not. You can tell the truth, or not. You can be kind, generous, and obedient. Or not.

Today, the world will offer you countless opportunities to let down your guard and, by doing so, let the devil do his worst. So be watchful and obedient. Guard your heart by giving it to your Heavenly Father; it is safe with Him.

Summing it all up, friends, I'd say you'll do best by filling your minds and meditating on things true, noble, reputable, authentic, compelling, gracious, the best, not the worst; the beautiful, not the ugly; things to praise, not things to curse. Put into practice what you learned from me, what you heard and saw and realized. Do that, and God, who makes everything work together, will work you into his most excellent harmonies.

Philippians 4:8-9 MSG

Prayer is our pathway not only to divine protection, but also to a personal, intimate relationship with God.

Shirley Dobson

Do nothing that you would not like to be doing when Jesus comes. Go no place where you would not like to be found when He returns.

Corrie ten Boom

If you're not sure what to do . . . slow down and listen to your conscience. That little voice inside your head is remarkably dependable, but you can't depend upon it if you never listen to it. So stop, listen, and learn—your conscience is almost always right!

Day 50

Today's Big Question About Putting God First

Question:

What does the Bible say about the place that God should occupy in your life and your heart?

Answer:

God's Word is clear: If you put Him first in every aspect of your life, you'll be blessed. But if you relegate God to a position of lesser importance, you'll distance yourself from His blessings.

If you want to figure out who you are—and who you want to become—you should be aware that self-understanding, like every other good thing in this universe, starts with God. In other words, you can't have a healthy relationship with yourself until you have a healthy relationship with your Creator.

As you think about the nature of your relationship with God, remember this: you will always have some type of relationship with Him—it is inevitable that your life must be lived in relationship to God. The question is not if you will have a relationship with Him; the burning question is whether or not that relationship will be one that seeks to honor Him.

Are you willing to place God first in your life? And, are you willing to welcome God's Son into your heart? Unless you can honestly answer these questions with a resounding yes, then your relationship with God isn't what it could be or should be. Thankfully, God is always available, He's always ready to forgive, and He's waiting to hear from you now. The rest, of course, is up to you.

Jesus answered, "'Love the Lord your God with all your heart, all your soul, and all your mind.' This is the first and most important command."

Matthew 22:37-38 NCV

Whatever you love most, be it sports, pleasure, business or God, that is your god.

Billy Graham

You must never sacrifice your relationship with God for the sake of a relationship with another person.

Charles Stanley

Today, spend a few minutes thinking about your relationship with God. Is it really an intimate one-on-one connection, or are you allowing other things to come between you and your Creator? Write down three specific steps that you can take right now to forge a stronger bond with your God.

Day 51

Today's Big Question About Your Example

Question:

What does the Bible say about the example that you should set for others?

Answer:

Your life is a sermon, so preach carefully. Remember that the words you choose to speak may have some impact on others, but not nearly as much impact as the life you choose to live.

All of us are examples—examples that should be emulated . . . or not. Hopefully, the lives we lead and the choices we make will serve as enduring examples of the spiritual abundance that is available to all who worship God and obey His commandments.

Ask yourself this question: Are you the kind of role model that you would want to emulate? If so, congratulations. But if certain aspects of your behavior could stand improvement, the best day to begin your self-improvement regimen is this one. Because whether you realize it or not, people you love are watching your behavior, and they're learning how to live. You owe it to them—and to yourself—to live righteously and well.

It is God's will that your good lives should silence those who make foolish accusations against you. You are not slaves; you are free. But your freedom is not an excuse to do evil. You are free to live as God's slaves.

I Peter 2:15-16 NLT

The sermon of your life in tough times ministers to people more powerfully than the most eloquent speaker.

Bill Bright

Living life with a consistent spiritual walk deeply influences those we love most.

Vonette Bright

In our faith we follow in someone's steps.
In our faith we leave footprints to guide others.
It's the principle of discipleship.

Max Lucado

Your life is a sermon. What kind of sermon will you preach? The words you choose to speak may have some impact on others, but not nearly as much impact as the life you choose to live.

Today's Big Question About Faith

Question:

What does the Bible say about the power of faith?

Answer:

Faith can move mountains. And faith is contagious. So act, pray, praise, and trust God with the certain knowledge that your friends and family are watching.

Because we live in a demanding world, all of us have mountains to climb and mountains to move. Moving those mountains requires faith.

Are you a mountain-moving Christian whose faith is evident for all to see? Or, are you a spiritual underachiever? As you think about the answer to that question, consider this: God needs more people who are willing to move mountains for His glory and for His kingdom.

Are you willing to let God help you move mountains, or are you still stumbling around over a few little molehills? The answer should be obvious. And so, with no more delays, let the mountain moving begin.

For I assure you: If you have faith the size of a mustard seed, you will tell this mountain, "Move from here to there," and it will move. Nothing will be impossible for you.

Matthew 17:20 HCSB

We are never stronger than the moment we admit we are weak.

Beth Moore

A faith that hasn't been tested can't be trusted.

Adrian Rogers

Faith never knows where it is being led, but it loves and knows the One Who is leading.

Oswald Chambers

Great hopes make great men.

Thomas Fuller

Faith should be practiced more than studied. Vance Havner said, "Nothing is more disastrous than to study faith, analyze faith, make noble resolves of faith, but never actually to make the leap of faith." How true!

Day 53

Today's Big Question About Fear of Failure

Question:

The fear of failure can be very real and very disturbing. So what should you do?

Answer:

Don't overestimate the consequences of failing. Remember that failing isn't nearly as bad as failing to try.

As we consider the uncertainties of the future, we are confronted with a powerful temptation: the temptation to "play it safe." Unwilling to move mountains, we fret over molehills. Unwilling to entertain great hopes for the tomorrow, we focus on the unfairness of the today. Unwilling to trust God completely, we take timid half-steps when God intends that we make giant leaps.

Today, ask God for the courage to step beyond the boundaries of your doubts. Ask Him to guide you to a place where you can realize your full potential—a place where you are freed from the fear of failure. Ask Him to do His part, and promise Him that you will do your part. Don't ask Him to lead you to a "safe" place; ask Him to lead you to the "right" place . . . and remember: those two places are seldom the same.

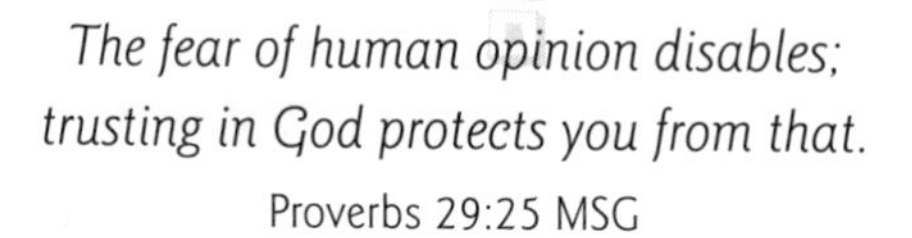

The fear of human opinion disables;
trusting in God protects you from that.

Proverbs 29:25 MSG

Far better it is to dare mighty things, to win glorious triumphs, even though checkered by failure, than to take rank with those poor spirits who neither enjoy much nor suffer much, because they live in the gray twilight that knows neither victory nor defeat.

Theodore Roosevelt

How beautiful it is to learn that grace isn't fragile, and that in the family of God we can fail and not be a failure.

Gloria Gaither

Let us arm ourselves against our spiritual enemies with courage. They think twice about engaging with one who fights boldly.

St. John Climacus

If you're too afraid of failure, you may not live up to your potential. So don't be too afraid to try.

Day 54

Today's Big Question About Following Christ

Question:

What does the Bible say about following in Jesus' footsteps?

Answer:

If you want to follow in Christ's footsteps . . . welcome Him into your heart, obey His commandments, and share His never-ending love.

Life is a series of choices. Each day, we make countless decisions that can bring us closer to God . . . or not. When we live according to God's commandments, we reap bountiful rewards: abundance, hope, and peace, for starters. But, when we turn our backs upon God by disobeying Him, we bring needless suffering upon ourselves and our families.

Do you seek to walk in the footsteps of the One from Galilee, or will you choose another path? If you sincerely seek God's peace and His blessings, then you must strive to imitate God's Son.

Thomas Brooks spoke for believers of every generation when he observed, "Christ is the sun, and all the watches of our lives should be set by the dial of his motion." Christ, indeed, is the ultimate Savior of mankind and the personal Savior of those who believe in Him. As His servants, we should walk in His footsteps as we share His love and His message with a world that needs both.

But whoever keeps His word, truly in him the love of God is perfected. This is how we know we are in Him: the one who says he remains in Him should walk just as He walked.

I John 2:5-6 HCSB

Jesus never asks us to give Him what we don't have. But He does demand that we give Him all we do have if we want to be a part of what He wishes to do in the lives of those around us!

Anne Graham Lotz

We have in Jesus Christ a perfect example of how to put God's truth into practice.

Bill Bright

You don't have to be perfect to follow in Christ's footsteps. Jesus doesn't expect your perfection—He expects your participation.

Day 55

Today's Big Question About Forgiveness

Question:

Sometimes it's very hard for me to forgive. What does the Bible say about forgiveness?

Answer:

Forgive . . . and keep forgiving! Sometimes, you may forgive someone once and then, at a later time, become angry at the very same person again. If so, you must forgive that person again and again . . . until it sticks!

Are you the kind of person who has a tough time forgiving and forgetting? If so, welcome to the club. Most of us find it difficult to forgive the people who have hurt us. And that's too bad because life would be much simpler if we could forgive people "once and for all" and be done with it. Yet forgiveness is seldom that easy. Usually, the decision to forgive is straightforward, but the process of forgiving is more difficult. Forgiveness is a journey that requires effort, time, perseverance, and prayer.

If there exists even one person whom you have not forgiven (and that includes yourself), obey God's commandment: forgive that person today. And remember that bitterness, anger, and regret are not part of God's plan for your life. Forgiveness is.

If you sincerely wish to forgive someone, pray for that person. And then pray for yourself by asking God to heal your heart. Don't expect forgiveness to be easy or quick, but rest assured: with God as your partner, you can forgive . . . and you will.

You have heard that it was said, You shall love your neighbor and hate your enemy. But I tell you, love your enemies, and pray for those who persecute you.

Matthew 5:43-44 HCSB

God expects us to forgive others as He has forgiven us; we are to follow His example by having a forgiving heart.

Vonette Bright

To be a Christian means to forgive the inexcusable, because God has forgiven the inexcusable in you.

C. S. Lewis

Forgive . . . and keep forgiving! Sometimes, you may forgive someone once and then, at a later time, become angry at the very same person again. If so, you must forgive that person again and again . . . until it sticks!

Day 56

Today's Big Question About God's Plan

Question:

What does the Bible say about God's plans for you?

Answer:

The Bible promises that God has a wonderful plan for you and your loved ones. And the time to start looking for that plan—and living it—is now. Discovering God's plan begins with prayer, but it doesn't end there. You've also got to work at it.

You'll feel better about yourself if you're living on purpose, not by accident. But sometimes that's hard to do. Why? Because God's plans aren't always clear.

Sometimes we wander aimlessly in a wilderness of our own making. And sometimes, we struggle mightily against God in an unsuccessful attempt to find success and happiness through our own means, not His.

Are you genuinely trying to figure out God's purpose for your life? If so, you can be sure that with God's help, you will eventually discover it. So keep praying, and keep watching. And rest assured: God's got big plans for you . . . very big plans.

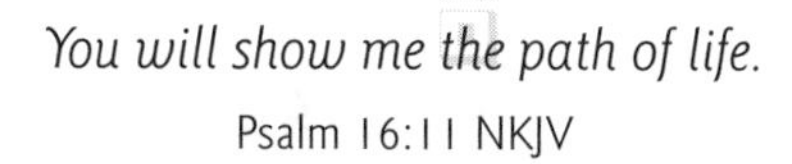
You will show me the path of life.

Psalm 16:11 NKJV

With God, it's never "Plan B" or "second best."
It's always "Plan A." And, if we let Him,
He'll make something beautiful of our lives.

Gloria Gaither

God is preparing you as his chosen arrow.
As yet your shaft is hidden in his quiver, in the shadows,
but, at the precise moment, he will reach for you
and launch you to that place of his appointment.

Charles Swindoll

If not a sparrow falls upon the ground without your Father,
you have reason to see that the smallest events of your
career and your life are arranged by him.

C. H. Spurgeon

God has very big plans in store for your life, so trust Him and wait patiently for those plans to unfold. And remember: God's timing is best.

Day 57

Today's Big Question About God's Timetable

Question:

Sometimes you're probably impatient for life to unfold. What does the Bible say about God's timing?

Answer:

God has very big plans in store for your life, so trust Him and wait patiently for those plans to unfold. And remember: God's timing is best, so don't allow yourself to become discouraged if things don't work out exactly as you wish. Instead of worrying about your future, entrust it to God. He knows exactly what you need and exactly when you need it.

Are you anxious for God to work out His plan for your life? Who isn't? As believers, we all want God to do great things for us and through us, and we want Him to do those things now. But sometimes, God has other plans. Sometimes, God's timetable does not coincide with our own. It's worth noting, however, that God's timetable is always perfect.

The next time you find your patience tested to the limit, remember that the world unfolds according to God's plan, not ours. Sometimes, we must wait patiently, and that's as it should be. After all, think how patient God has been with us.

He has made everything appropriate in its time.
He has also put eternity in their hearts, but man cannot discover the work God has done from beginning to end.

Ecclesiastes 3:11 HCSB

Your times are in His hands.
He's in charge of the timetable, so wait patiently.

Kay Arthur

God has a designated time when his promise will be fulfilled and the prayer will be answered.

Jim Cymbala

When there is perplexity there is always guidance—not always at the moment we ask, but in good time, which is God's time. There is no need to fret and stew.

Elisabeth Elliot

You have a timetable, and God has a timetable. Remember that His is better than yours.

Day 58

Today's Big Question About Humility

Question:

What does the Bible say about humility?

Answer:

God favors the humble just as surely as He disciplines the proud. So you must remain humble or face the consequences. Pride does go before the fall, but humility often prevents the fall.

On the road to spiritual growth, pride is a massive roadblock. The more prideful you are, the more difficult it is to know God. When you experience success, it's easy to puff out your chest and proclaim, "I did that!" But it's wrong. Dietrich Bonhoeffer was correct when he observed, "It is very easy to overestimate the importance of our own achievements in comparison with what we owe others." In other words, reality breeds humility. So if you want to know God better, be humble. Otherwise, you'll be building a roadblock between you and your Creator (and that's a very bad thing to do!).

Therefore humble yourselves under the mighty hand of God, that He may exalt you in due time.

I Peter 5:6 NKJV

We are never stronger than the moment we admit we are weak.

Beth Moore

Do you wish to rise? Begin by descending. You plan a tower that will pierce the clouds? Lay first the foundation of humility.

St. Augustine

Nothing sets a person so much out of the devil's reach as humility.

Jonathan Edwards

Do you value humility above status? If so, God will smile upon your endeavors. But if you value status above humility, you're inviting God's displeasure. In short, humility pleases God; pride does not.

Day 59

Today's Big Question About Materialism

Question:

We live in a materialistic world. What does the Bible have to say about that?

Answer:

Too much stuff doesn't ensure happiness. In fact, having too much stuff can actually prevent happiness.

How important are our material possessions? Not as important as we might think. In a well-balanced life, material possessions should play a rather small role. Of course, we all need the basic necessities of life, but once we meet those needs for ourselves and for our families, the piling up of possessions often creates more problems than it solves. Our real riches are not of this world. We are never really rich until we are rich in spirit.

If you've become preoccupied with money and the things that money can buy, it's time to de-emphasize things material and re-emphasize things spiritual. When you do, you'll feel better about yourself . . . and you'll begin storing up riches that will endure forever: the spiritual kind.

And He told them, "Watch out and be on guard against all greed, because one's life is not in the abundance of his possessions."

Luke 12:15 HCSB

A society that pursues pleasure runs the risk of raising expectations ever higher, so that true contentment always lies tantalizingly out of reach.

Philip Yancey and Paul Brand

It's sobering to contemplate how much time, effort, sacrifice, compromise, and attention we give to acquiring and increasing our supply of something that is totally insignificant in eternity.

Anne Graham Lotz

The more we stuff ourselves with material pleasures, the less we seem to appreciate life.

Barbara Johnson

If you find yourself focusing too much on stuff, try spending a little less time at the mall and a little more time talking to God.

Day 60

Today's Big Question About Miracles

Question:

Sometimes, it can be hard to believe in miracles. What assurances can be found in the Bible?

Answer:

If you're looking for miracles . . . you'll find them. If you're not, you won't.

One way we can strengthen our faith is by looking carefully at the miraculous things that God does. But sometimes, we're simply too preoccupied to notice. Instead of paying careful attention to God's handiwork, we become distracted. Instead of expecting God to work miracles, we become cynical. Instead of depending on God's awesome power, we seek to muddle along using our own power—with decidedly mixed results.

Miracles, both great and small, are an integral part of everyday life—and they are a part of your life, too. But here's the million-dollar question: have you noticed?

If you lack the faith that God can work miracles in your own life, it's time to reconsider. Instead of doubting God, trust His power, and expect His miracles. Then, wait patiently . . . because something miraculous is about to happen.

God verified the message by signs and wonders and various miracles and by giving gifts of the Holy Spirit whenever he chose to do so.

Hebrews 2:4 NLT

The healing acts of Jesus were themselves a message that he had come to set men free.

Francis MacNutt

When God is involved, anything can happen. Be open and stay that way. God has a beautiful way of bringing good vibrations out of broken chords.

Charles Swindoll

I could go through this day oblivious to the miracles all around me or I could tune in and "enjoy."

Gloria Gaither

God has infinite power. If you're watchful, you'll observe many miracles. So keep your eyes, your heart, and your mind open.

Day 61

Today's Big Question About Perfectionism

Question:

What does the Bible say about perfectionism?

Answer:

All have sinned, and nobody is perfect. So don't be too hard on yourself: you don't have to be perfect to be wonderful.

Expectations, expectations, expectations! The media delivers an endless stream of messages that tell you how to look, how to behave, and how to dress. The media's expectations are impossible to meet—God's are not. God doesn't expect perfection . . . and neither should you.

If you find yourself bound up by the chains of perfectionism, it's time to ask yourself who you're trying to impress, and why. If you're trying to impress other people, it's time to reconsider your priorities. Your first responsibility is to the Heavenly Father who created you and to His Son who saved you. Then, you bear a powerful responsibility to your family. But, when it comes to meeting society's unrealistic expectations, forget it!

Remember that when you accepted Christ as your Savior, God accepted you for all eternity. Now, it's your turn to accept yourself and your loved ones. When you do, you'll feel a tremendous weight being lifted from your shoulders. After all, pleasing God is simply a matter of obeying His commandments and accepting His Son. But as for pleasing everybody else? That's impossible!

Those who wait for perfect weather will never plant seeds; those who look at every cloud will never harvest crops. Plant early in the morning, and work until evening, because you don't know if this or that will succeed. They might both do well.

Ecclesiastes 11:4, 6 NCV

What makes a Christian a Christian is not perfection but forgiveness.

Max Lucado

It is comfortable to know that we are responsible to God and not to man. It is a small matter to be judged of man's judgement.

Lottie Moon

Don't be too hard on yourself: you don't have to be perfect to be wonderful.

Day 62

Today's Big Question About Rejection

Question:

Handling rejection is tough. What does the Bible say about it?

Answer:

God's Word teaches us to worry more about pleasing God and less about pleasing people. So keep things in perspective by remembering that a little rejection isn't really such a big deal.

If you're like most people, you're sensitive to rejection. But you should be aware that the fear of rejection can be a major roadblock on the path to a purposeful life. Why? Because the more fearful you are of displeasing others, the more likely you are to make decisions that are not in your best interest.

When you try to please everybody in sight, you create for yourself a task that is unrealistic, unsatisfying, and unworthy of your efforts. A far better strategy, of course, is to concentrate, first and foremost, on pleasing God. But sometimes, that's easier said than done, especially if you focus too intently on being a "people pleaser."

So, focus your thoughts and energies on pleasing your Creator first and always. And when it comes to the world and all its inhabitants, don't worry too much about the folks you can't please. Focus, instead, on doing the right thing—and leave the rest up to God.

Wherever they do not welcome you,
when you leave that town, shake off the dust from your feet
as a testimony against them.

Luke 9:5 HCSB

The enemy of our souls loves to taunt us with past failures, wrongs, disappointments, disasters, and calamities. And if we let him continue doing this, our life becomes a long and dark tunnel, with very little light at the end.

Charles Swindoll

A healthy self-identity is seeing yourself as God sees you—no more and no less.

Josh McDowell

If you're feeling discouraged, try to redirect your thoughts away from the troubles that plague you—focus, instead, upon the opportunities that surround you.

Day 63

Today's Big Question About Christ's Love

Question:

What should Christ's love mean to you?

Answer:

Jesus loves me, this I know . . . but how much? Here's how much: Jesus loves you so much that He gave His life so that you might live forever with Him in heaven. And how can you repay Christ's love? By accepting Him into your heart and by obeying His rules. When you do, He will love you and bless you today, tomorrow, and forever.

How much does Christ love us? More than we, as mere mortals, can comprehend. His love is perfect and steadfast. Even though we are imperfect and wayward, the Good Shepherd cares for us still. Even though we have fallen far short of the Father's commandments, Christ loves us with a power and depth that are beyond our understanding. The sacrifice that Jesus made upon the cross was made for each of us, and His love endures to the edge of eternity and beyond.

Christ's love changes everything, including your relationships. When you accept His gift of grace, you are transformed, not only for today, but also for all eternity.

For I am persuaded that neither death nor life, nor angels nor rulers, nor things present, nor things to come, nor powers, nor height, nor depth, nor any other created thing will have the power to separate us from the love of God that is in Christ Jesus our Lord!

Romans 8:38-39 HCSB

Live your lives in love, the same sort of love which Christ gives us, and which He perfectly expressed when He gave Himself as a sacrifice to God.

Corrie ten Boom

God expressed His love in sending the Holy Spirit to live within us.

Charles Stanley

God is my heavenly Father. He loves me with an everlasting love. The proof of that is the Cross.

Elisabeth Elliot

Jesus loves you . . . His love is amazing, it's wonderful, and it's meant for you.

Day 64

Today's Big Question About Discipleship

Question:

What does the Bible say about discipleship?

Answer:

God's Word instructs you to follow in Christ's footsteps. And when it comes to discipleship, you owe it, not just to yourself or to God, but also to your family, to be a devoted follower of the One from Galilee.

When Jesus addressed His disciples, He warned that each one must, "take up his cross and follow Me." The disciples must have known exactly what the Master meant. In Jesus' day, prisoners were forced to carry their own crosses to the location where they would be put to death. Thus, Christ's message was clear: in order to follow Him, Christ's disciples must deny themselves and, instead, trust Him completely. Nothing has changed since then.

If we are to be disciples of Christ, we must trust Him and place Him at the very center of our beings. Jesus never comes "next." He is always first.

Do you seek to be a worthy disciple of Christ? Then pick up His cross today and every day that you live. When you do, He will bless you now and forever.

He has told you men what is good and what it is the Lord requires of you: Only to act justly, to love faithfulness, and to walk humbly with your God.

Micah 6:8 HCSB

Discipleship means allegiance to the suffering Christ, and it is therefore not at all surprising that Christians should be called upon to suffer.

Dietrich Bonhoeffer

Discipleship is a daily discipline: we follow Jesus a step at a time, a day at a time.

Warren Wiersbe

Discipleship is a decision to live by what I know about God, not by what I feel about him or myself or my neighbors.

Eugene Peterson

Jesus has invited you to become His disciple. If you accept His invitation—and if you obey His commandments—you will be protected and blessed.

Day 65

Today's Big Question About God's Power and Your Possibilities

Question:

What does the Bible say about God's power?

Answer:

God can do anything, and He can work miracles in your own life if you let Him.

Is your faith a little threadbare and worn? If so, it's time to abandon your doubts and reclaim your faith in God's promises.

Ours is a God of infinite possibilities. But sometimes, because of limited faith and limited understanding, we wrongly assume that God cannot or will not intervene in the affairs of mankind. Such assumptions are simply wrong.

God's Holy Word makes it clear: absolutely nothing is impossible for the Lord. And since the Bible means what it says, you can be comforted in the knowledge that the Creator of the universe can do miraculous things in your own life and in the lives of your loved ones. Your challenge, as a believer, is to take God at His word, and to expect the miraculous.

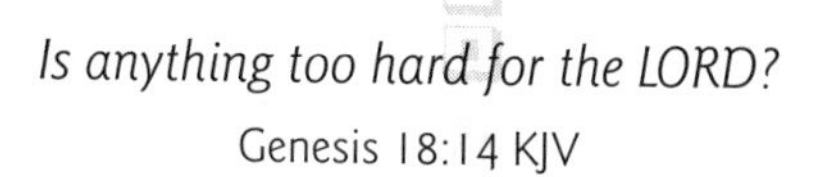

Is anything too hard for the LORD?

Genesis 18:14 KJV

The task ahead of us is never as great as the Power behind us.

Anonymous

If we take God's program, we can have God's power—
not otherwise.

E. Stanley Jones

You can believe in the Holy Spirit not because you see Him, but because you see what He does in people's lives when they are surrendered to Christ and possess His power.

Billy Graham

No giant will ever be a match for a big God with a little rock.

Beth Moore

Today, as a way of managing stress, think of all the wonderful things that God has done for you. And then, take time to ponder His promises for the future. When you focus on God's gifts, you won't stay stressed for long.

Day 66

Today's Big Question About Problems

Question:
Everybody (including you) has problems. What can God's Word teach about your problems?

Answer:
When it comes to solving problems, work beats worry. Remember: It is better to fix than to fret.

Life is an adventure in problem-solving. When it comes to solving the problems of everyday living, we often know precisely what needs to be done, but we may be slow in doing it—especially if what needs to be done is difficult. So we put off till tomorrow what should be done today.

As a young person living here in today's world, you have your own set of challenges. As you face those challenges, you may be comforted by this fact: Trouble, of every kind, is temporary. Yet God's grace is eternal. And worries, of every kind, are temporary. But God's love is everlasting. The troubles that concern you will pass. God remains. And for every problem, God has a solution.

The words of Psalm 34 remind us that the Lord solves problems for "people who do what is right." And usually, doing "what is right" means doing the uncomfortable work of confronting our problems sooner rather than later.

People who do what is right may have many problems,
but the Lord will solve them all.

Psalm 34:19 NCV

Hope looks for the good in people, opens doors for people,
discovers what can be done to help, lights a candle,
does not yield to cynicism. Hope sets people free.

Barbara Johnson

Life will be made or broken at the place
where we meet and deal with obstacles.

E. Stanley Jones

Keep your feet on the ground, but let your heart soar
as high as it will. Refuse to be average or to surrender
to the chill of your spiritual environment.

A. W. Tozer

Remember that "this, too, will pass." And remember that it will pass more quickly if you spend more time solving problems and less time fretting over them.

Day 67

Today's Big Question About Finding Purpose

Question:

What does the Bible say about the search for purpose and meaning?

Answer:

God has a wonderful plan for you, and discovering that plan requires a willingness to be open. God's plan is unfolding day by day. If you keep your eyes and your heart open, He'll reveal His plans. God has big things in store for you, but He may have quite a few lessons to teach you before you are fully prepared to do His will and fulfill His purposes.

God has things He wants you to do and places He wants you to go. The most important decision of your life is, of course, your commitment to accept Jesus Christ as your personal Lord and Savior. And, once your eternal destiny is secured, you will undoubtedly ask yourself the question "What now, Lord?" If you earnestly seek God's will for your life, you will find it . . . in time.

As you seek to discover God's path for your life, you should study His Holy Word and be ever watchful for His signs. You should associate with fellow Christians who will encourage your spiritual growth, and you should listen to that inner voice that speaks to you in the quiet moments of your daily devotionals.

Rest assured: God is here, and He intends to use you in wonderful, unexpected ways. He desires to lead you along a path of His choosing. Your challenge is to watch, to listen . . . and to follow.

You will show me the path of life; in Your presence is fullness of joy; at Your right hand are pleasures forevermore.

Psalm 16:11 NKJV

Only God's chosen task for you will ultimately satisfy. Do not wait until it is too late to realize the privilege of serving Him in His chosen position for you.

Beth Moore

In the very place where God has put us, whatever its limitations, whatever kind of work it may be, we may indeed serve the Lord Christ.

Elisabeth Elliot

God has a plan for your life, a definite purpose that you can fulfill . . . or not. Your challenge is to pray for God's guidance and to follow wherever He leads.

Day 68

Today's Big Question About Praise

Question:

What does the Bible teach us about praising God?

Answer:

It always pays to praise your Creator. That's why thoughtful believers (like you) make it a habit to carve out quiet moments throughout the day to praise God.

If you're like most people on the planet, you're very busy. Your life is probably hectic, demanding, and complicated. When the demands of life leave you rushing from place to place with scarcely a moment to spare, you may fail to pause and thank your Creator for the blessings He has bestowed upon you. Big mistake.

No matter how busy you are, you should never be too busy to thank God for His gifts. Your task, as an extreme follower of the living Christ, is to praise God many times each day. After all, your Heavenly Father has blessed you beyond measure, and you owe Him everything, including your thanks, starting now.

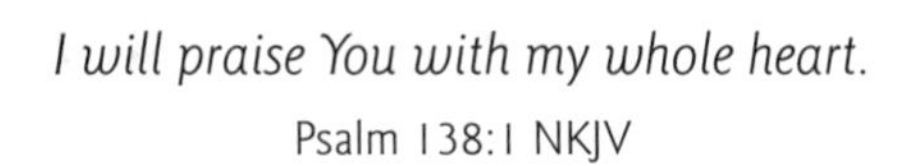

I will praise You with my whole heart.

Psalm 138:1 NKJV

Two wings are necessary to lift our souls toward God: prayer and praise. Prayer asks. Praise accepts the answer.

Mrs. Charles E. Cowman

Praise opens the window of our hearts, preparing us to walk more closely with God. Prayer raises the window of our spirit, enabling us to listen more clearly to the Father.

Max Lucado

Be not afraid of saying too much in the praises of God; all the danger is of saying too little.

Matthew Henry

Praise Him! One of the big reasons you should attend church is to praise God. But, you need not wait until Sunday rolls around to thank your Heavenly Father. Instead, you can praise Him many times each day by saying silent prayers that only He can hear.

Day 69

Today's Big Question About Prayer

Question:

What does the Bible say about prayer?

Answer:

One way to make sure that your heart is in tune with God is to pray early and often. The more you talk to God, the more He will talk to you.

Perhaps, because of your demanding schedule, you've neglected to pay sufficient attention to a particularly important part of your life: the spiritual part. If so, today is the day to change, and one way to make that change is simply to spend a little more time talking with God.

God is trying to get His message through to you. Are you listening?

Perhaps, on occasion, you may find yourself overwhelmed by the press of everyday life. Perhaps you may forget to slow yourself down long enough to talk with God. Instead of turning your thoughts and prayers to Him, you may rely upon our own resources. Instead of asking God for guidance, you may depend only upon your own limited wisdom. A far better course of action is this: simply stop what you're doing long enough to open your heart to God; then listen carefully for His directions.

In all things great and small, seek God's wisdom and His grace. He hears your prayers, and He will answer. All you must do is ask.

Rejoice always! Pray constantly. Give thanks in everything, for this is God's will for you in Christ Jesus.

I Thessalonians 5:16-18 HCSB

We must pray literally without ceasing, in every occurrence and employment of our lives. You know I mean that prayer of the heart which is independent of place or situation, or which is, rather, a habit of lifting up the heart to God, as in a constant communication with Him.

Elizabeth Ann Seton

Do nothing at all unless you begin with prayer.

Ephraem the Syrian

Of course you should pray at mealtime and bedtime, but that's just the beginning. You can offer lots of prayers to God all day long . . . and you should!

Day 70

Today's Big Question About Temptations

Question:

This world is filled with temptations. What should you do?

Answer:

At every turn in the road, or so it seems, somebody is trying to tempt you with something. Your job is to steer clear of temptation . . . and to keep steering clear as long as you live. Remember the old saying: "When it comes to temptation, it's easier to stay out than it is to get out."

Face facts: you live in a temptation-filled world. The devil is hard at work in your neighborhood, and so are his helpers. Here in the 21st century, the bad guys are working around the clock to lead you astray. That's why you must remain vigilant.

In a letter to believers, Peter offers a stern warning: "Your adversary, the devil, prowls around like a roaring lion, seeking someone to devour" (I Peter 5:8 NASB). What was true in New Testament times is equally true in our own. Satan tempts his prey and then devours them (and it's up to you—and only you—to make sure that you're not one of the ones being devoured!).

As a believer who seeks a radical relationship with Jesus, you must beware because temptations are everywhere. Satan is determined to win; you must be equally determined that he does not.

Put on the whole armor of God,
that you may be able to stand against the wiles of the devil.
Ephesians 6:11 NKJV

Jesus faced every temptation known to humanity
so that He could identify with us.
Beth Moore

Our battles are first won or lost in the secret places
of our will in God's presence, never in full view of the world.
Oswald Chambers

Flee temptation without leaving a forwarding address.
Barbara Johnson

Temptations are everywhere. It's your job to avoid them . . . or else!

Day 71

Today's Big Question About Trusting God

Question:

Sometimes it's hard to trust God. What does the Bible say about that?

Answer:

It's simple: depend upon God. Remember the words of Vance Havner: "We must live in all kinds of days, both high days and low days, in simple dependence upon Christ as the branch on the vine. This is the supreme experience."

Sometimes the future seems bright, and sometimes it does not. Yet even when we cannot see the possibilities of tomorrow, God can. As believers, our challenge is to trust an uncertain future to an all-powerful God.

When we trust God, we should trust Him without reservation. We should steel ourselves against the inevitable stresses of the day, secure in the knowledge that our Heavenly Father has a plan for the future that only He can see.

Can you place your future into the hands of a loving and all-knowing God? Can you live amid the uncertainties of today, knowing that God has dominion over all your tomorrows? If you can, you are wise and you are blessed. When you trust God with everything you are and everything you have, He will bless you now and forever.

It is better to trust the Lord than to put confidence in people.
It is better to trust the Lord than to put confidence in princes.

Psalm 118:8-9 NLT

Conditions are always changing; therefore,
I must not be dependent upon conditions.
What matters supremely is my soul and
my relationship to God.

Corrie ten Boom

True faith is man's weakness leaning on God's strength.

D. L. Moody

Sometimes the very essence of faith is trusting God
in the midst of things He knows good
and well we cannot comprehend.

Beth Moore

One of the most important lessons that you can ever learn is to trust God for everything—not some things, not most things . . . everything! The more you trust God, the more easily you can overcome the inevitable stresses of everyday life.

Today's Big Question About The World's Values

Question:

The world is filled with distractions and temptations. What should you do?

Answer:

It's simple: Pay less attention to the world's promises and more attention to God's promises.

Our world is filled with pressures: some good, some bad. The pressures that we feel to follow God's will and obey His commandments are positive pressures. God places them on our hearts so that we might act in accordance with His will. But we also face different pressures, ones that are definitely not from God. When we feel pressured to do things—or even to think thoughts—that lead us away from Him, we must beware.

Many elements of society seek to mold us into more worldly beings; God, on the other hand, seeks to mold us into new beings, new creations through Christ, beings that are most certainly not conformed to this world. If we are to please God, we must resist the pressures that society seeks to impose upon us, and we must conform ourselves, instead, to His will, to His path, and to His Son.

Don't love the world's ways. Don't love the world's goods. Love of the world squeezes out love for the Father. Practically everything that goes on in the world—wanting your own way, wanting everything for yourself, wanting to appear important—has nothing to do with the Father. It just isolates you from him. The world and all its wanting, wanting, wanting is on the way out—but whoever does what God wants is set for eternity.

1 John 2:15-17 MSG

He who dies with the most toys . . . still dies.

Anonymous

The only ultimate disaster that can befall us,
I have come to realize, is to feel ourselves
to be home on earth.

Max Lucado

The more we stuff ourselves with material pleasures,
the less we seem to appreciate life.

Barbara Johnson

The world makes plenty of promises that it can't keep. God, on the other hand, keeps every single one of His promises.

Day 73

Today's Big Question About Perseverance

Question:

If you're tempted to give up, what advice does the Bible have for you?

Answer:

The world encourages instant gratification, but God's work takes time. So remember the words of C. H. Spurgeon: "By perseverance, the snail reached the ark."

Do you sincerely want to live a life that is pleasing to God? If so, you must remember that life is not a sprint; it's a marathon that calls for preparation, determination, and lots of perseverance.

Are you one of those people who doesn't give up easily, or are you quick to bail out when the going gets tough? If you've developed the unfortunate habit of giving up at the first sign of trouble, it's probably time for you to have a heart-to-heart talk with the person you see every time you look in the mirror.

Jesus finished what He began, and so should you. Despite His suffering, despite the shame of the cross, Jesus was steadfast in His faithfulness to God. You, too, must remain faithful, especially when times are tough.

Do you want to build a closer relationship with God? Then don't give up. And if you're facing a difficult situation, remember this: whatever your problem, God can handle it. Your job is to keep persevering until He does.

So we must not get tired of doing good,
for we will reap at the proper time if we don't give up.

Galatians 6:9 HCSB

Every achievement worth remembering is stained with the blood of diligence and scarred by the wounds of disappointment.

Charles Swindoll

Keep adding, keep walking, keep advancing; do not stop, do not turn back, do not turn from the straight road.

St. Augustine

If things don't work out at first, don't quit. If you never try, you'll never know how good you can be.

Day 74

Today's Big Question About Silence

Question:

It's noisy out there. What does the Bible say about finding time for quiet reflection?

Answer:

Time and again, God's Word encourages believers to quiet themselves and spend silent moments with the Father. So begin each day with a few minutes of quiet time to organize your thoughts and praise your Creator.

When you have doubts, remember this: God isn't on a coffee break, and He hasn't moved out of town. God isn't taking a long vacation, and He isn't snoozing on the couch. He's right here, right now, listening to your thoughts and prayers, watching over your every move.

The Bible teaches that a wonderful way to get to know God is simply to be still and listen to Him. But sometimes, you may find it hard to slow down and listen. As the demands of everyday life weigh down upon you, you may be tempted to ignore God's presence or—worse yet—to rebel against His commandments. But, when you quiet yourself and acknowledge His presence, God touches your heart and restores your spirit. So why not let Him do it right now? If you really want to know Him better, silence is a wonderful place to start.

Be silent before the Lord and wait expectantly for Him.

Psalm 37:7 HCSB

There are times when to speak is to violate the moment—
when silence represents the highest respect.
The word for such times is reverence.

Max Lucado

Growth takes place in quietness, in hidden ways,
in silence and solitude.
The process is not accessible to observation.

Eugene Peterson

If you, too, will learn to wait upon God,
to get alone with Him, and remain silent so that
you can hear His voice when He is ready to speak to you,
what a difference it will make in your life!

Kay Arthur

You live in a noisy world filled with distractions, a world where silence is in short supply. But God wants you to carve out quiet moments with Him. Silence is, indeed, golden.

Day 75

Today's Big Question About The Power of Encouragement

Question:

So many people around me seem to need encouragement. What should I do?

Answer:

Do you want to be successful and go far in life? Encourage others to do the same. You can't lift other people up without lifting yourself up, too. And remember the words of Oswald Chambers: "God grant that we may not hinder those who are battling their way slowly into the light."

Here's a question only you can answer: During a typical day, how many opportunities will you have to encourage other human beings? Unless you're living on a deserted island, the answer is "a lot!" And here's a follow-up question: How often do you take advantage of those opportunities? Hopefully, the answer is "more often than not."

Romans 14:19 advises us to "Pursue what promotes peace and what builds up one another" (HCSB). And whenever we do, God smiles.

Whether you realize it or not, you're surrounded by people who need an encouraging word, a helping hand, or a pat on the back. And every time you encourage one of these folks, you'll being doing God's will by obeying God's Word. So with no further ado, let the encouragement begin.

Patience and encouragement come from God.
And I pray that God will help you all agree
with each other the way Christ Jesus wants.

Romans 15:5 NCV

Giving encouragement to others is a most welcome gift,
for the results of it are lifted spirits,
increased self-worth, and a hopeful future.

Florence Littauer

I can usually sense that a leading is from the Holy Spirit when it calls me to humble myself, to serve somebody, to encourage somebody, or to give something away. Very rarely will the evil one lead us to do those kind of things.

Bill Hybels

Encouragement is contagious. You can't lift other people up without lifting yourself up, too.

Day 76

Today's Big Question About Patience

Question:

Sometimes it's hard to be patient. What advice can be found in God's Word?

Answer:

God's Word teaches that patience is better than strength (Proverbs 16:32). So wise people learn to control anger before anger controls them.

Are you a perfectly patient person? If so, feel free to skip the rest of this page. But if you're not, here's something to think about: If you really want to become a more patient person, God is ready and willing to help.

The Bible promises that when you sincerely seek God's help, He will give you the things that you need—and that includes patience. But God won't force you to become a more patient person. If you want to become a more mature Christian, you've got to do some of the work yourself—and the best time to start doing that work is now.

So, if you want to gain patience and maturity, bow your head and start praying about it. Then, rest assured that with God's help, you can most certainly make yourself a more patient, understanding, mature Christian.

Be gentle to everyone, able to teach, and patient.

2 Timothy 2:23 HCSB

Be patient. God is using today's difficulties to strengthen you for tomorrow. He is equipping you.
The God who makes things grow will help you bear fruit.

Max Lucado

You can't step in front of God and not get in trouble.
When He says, "Go three steps," don't go four.

Charles Stanley

The deepest spiritual lessons are not learned by His letting us have our way in the end, but by His making us wait, bearing with us in love and patience until we are able honestly to pray what He taught His disciples to pray: Thy will be done.

Elisabeth Elliot

Want other people to be patient with you? Then you must do the same for them. Never expect other people to be more patient with you than you are with them.

Day 77

Today's Big Question About Media Messages

Question:

Media messages are pretty warped. What does the Bible have to say about it?

Answer:

God's Word warns you to resist the world's values. So don't fall for the media's mixed-up messages. Instead of falling for the media's hype, focus on God's truth.

Sometimes it's hard being a Christian, especially when the world keeps pumping out messages that are contrary to your faith.

The media is working around the clock in an attempt to rearrange your priorities. The media says that your appearance is all-important, that your clothes are all-important, that your car is all-important, and that partying is all-important. But guess what? Those messages are lies. The important things in your life have little to do with parties or appearances. The all-important things in life have to do with your faith, your family, and your future. Period.

Are you willing to stand up for your faith? If so, you'll be doing yourself a king-sized favor. And consider this: When you begin to speak up for God, isn't it logical to assume that you'll also begin to know Him in a more meaningful way? Of course you will.

So do yourself a favor: forget the media hype, and pay attention to God. Stand up for Him and be counted, not just in church where it's relatively easy to be a Christian, but also outside the church, where it's significantly harder. You owe it God . . . and you owe it to yourself.

No one should deceive himself. If anyone among you thinks he is wise in this age, he must become foolish so that he can become wise. For the wisdom of this world is foolishness with God, since it is written: He catches the wise in their craftiness.

I Corinthians 3:18-19 HCSB

I have a divided heart, trying to love God
and the world at the same time. God says,
"You can't love me as you should if you love this world too."

Mary Morrison Suggs

The media is sending out messages that are dangerous to your physical, emotional, and spiritual health. If you choose to believe those messages, you're setting yourself up for lots of trouble.

Day 78

Today's Big Question About Worship

Question:

What does the Bible teach us about worship?

Answer:

The best way to worship God is to worship Him sincerely and often.

If you really want to know God, you must be willing to worship Him seven days a week, not just on Sunday.

God has a wonderful plan for your life, and an important part of that plan includes the time that you set aside for praise and worship. Every life, including yours, is based upon some form of worship. The question is not whether you will worship, but what you worship.

If you choose to worship God, you will receive a bountiful harvest of joy, peace, and abundance. But if you distance yourself from God by foolishly worshiping earthly possessions and personal gratification, you're making a huge mistake. So do this: Worship God today and every day. Worship Him with sincerity and thanksgiving. Write His name on your heart and rest assured that He, too, has written your name on His.

Worship the Lord your God and . . . serve Him only.

Matthew 4:10 HCSB

To worship Him in truth means to worship Him honestly,
without hypocrisy, standing open
and transparent before Him.

Anne Graham Lotz

Worship is a voluntary act of gratitude offered
by the saved to the Savior, by the healed to the Healer,
by the delivered to the Deliverer.

Max Lucado

Worship is spiritual. Our worship must be more
than just outward expression,
it must also take place in our spirits.

Franklin Graham

Worship is not meant to be boxed up in a church building on Sunday morning. To the contrary, praise and worship should be woven into the very fabric of your life.

Day 79

Today's Big Question About Happiness

Question:

What does the Bible have to say about happiness?

Answer:

Even if you're a very good person, you shouldn't expect to be happy all the time. Sometimes, things will happen to make you sad, and it's okay to be sad when bad things happen to you or to your friends and family. But remember: through good times and bad, you'll always be happier if you obey the rules of your Father in heaven. So obey them!

Do you sincerely want to be a happy Christian? Then set your mind and your heart upon God's love and His grace.

Happiness depends less upon our circumstances than upon our thoughts. When we turn our thoughts to God, to His gifts, and to His glorious creation, we experience the joy that God intends for His children. But, when we focus on the negative aspects of life, we suffer needlessly.

The fullness of life in Christ is available to all who seek it and claim it. Count yourself among that number. Seek first the salvation that is available through a personal relationship with Jesus Christ, and then claim the joy, the peace, and the spiritual abundance that the Shepherd offers His sheep.

Rejoice in the Lord always. I will say it again: Rejoice!

Philippians 4:4 HCSB

No matter how hard he searches,
nothing beneath the skies and nothing above the skies can
make any man happy apart from God.

C. H. Spurgeon

God has charged Himself with full responsibility
for our eternal happiness and stands ready to take over
the management of our lives the moment we turn
in faith to Him.

A. W. Tozer

Pleasure-seeking is a barren business; happiness is never
found till we have the grace to stop looking for it and to give
our attention to persons and matters external to ourselves.

J. I. Packer

The best day to be happy is this one. Don't spend your whole life in the waiting room. Make up your mind to celebrate today.

Day 30

Today's Big Question About God's Sufficiency

Question:

If you have challenges that seem overwhelming, what should you do?

Answer:

Turn to God. The Bible promises that He is sufficient to meet your every need.

It is easy to become overwhelmed by the demands of everyday life, but if you're a faithful follower, you need never be overwhelmed. Why? Because God's love is sufficient to meet your needs. Whatever dangers you may face, whatever heartbreaks you must endure, God is with you, and He stands ready to comfort you and to heal you.

The Psalmist writes, "Weeping may endure for a night, but joy comes in the morning" (Psalm 30:5 NKJV). But when we are suffering, the morning may seem very far away. It is not. God promises that He is "near to those who have a broken heart" (Psalm 34:18 NKJV).

If you are experiencing the intense pain of a recent loss, or if you are still mourning a loss from long ago, perhaps you are now ready to begin the next stage of your journey with God. If so, be mindful of this fact: the loving heart of God is sufficient to meet any challenge, including yours.

The Lord is my rock, my fortress, and my deliverer.

Psalm 18:2 HCSB

Faith is not merely you holding on to God—
it is God holding on to you.

E. Stanley Jones

God is always sufficient in perfect proportion to our need.

Beth Moore

God will call you to obey Him and do whatever he asks of you. However, you do not need to be doing something to feel fulfilled. You are fulfilled completely in a relationship with God. When you are filled with Him, what else do you need?

Henry Blackaby and Claude King

Focus on possibilities, not stumbling blocks. Of course you will encounter occasional disappointments, and, from time to time, you will encounter failure. But, don't invest large quantities of your life focusing on past misfortunes. Instead, look to the future with optimism and hope . . . and encourage your friends and family members to do the same.

Day 81

Today's Big Question About God's Presence

Question:

Sometimes God seems very far away. What does the Bible say about that?

Answer:

God isn't far away—He's right here, right now. And He's willing to talk to you right here, right now. So find a quiet place and open your heart to Him. When you do, you'll sense God's presence and His love, which, by the way, is already surrounding you and your loved ones.

Do you ever wonder if God really hears your prayers? If so, you're in good company: lots of very faithful Christians have wondered the same thing. In fact, some of the biggest heroes in the Bible had their doubts—and so, perhaps, will you. But when you have your doubts, remember this: God isn't on vacation, and He hasn't moved out of town. God isn't taking a coffee break, and He isn't snoozing on the couch. He's right here, right now, listening to your thoughts and prayers, watching over your every move.

As the demands of everyday life weigh down upon you, you may be tempted to ignore God's presence or—worse yet—to rebel against His commandments. But, when you quiet yourself and acknowledge His presence, God touches your heart and restores your spirits. So why not let Him do it right now?

I am not alone, because the Father is with Me.

John 16:32 HCSB

God walks with us. He scoops us up in His arms or simply sits with us in silent strength until we cannot avoid the awesome recognition that yes, even now, He is here.

Gloria Gaither

If you want to hear God's voice clearly and you are uncertain, then remain in His presence until He changes that uncertainty. Often, much can happen during this waiting for the Lord. Sometimes, he changes pride into humility, doubt into faith and peace.

Corrie ten Boom

If you're here, God is here. If you're there, God is, too. You can't get away from Him or His love . . . thank goodness!

Day 82

Today's Big Question About Perspective

Question:

When you're worried or stressed, it's easy to lose perspective. What should you do?

Answer:

Slow down, catch your breath, and have a chat with God. Your life is an integral part of God's grand plan. So don't be bothered by those minor inconveniences that are a part of everyday existence. Life is far too short, and besides, your friends and family are watching and learning . . . from you.

Sometimes, amid the demands of daily life, we lose perspective. Life seems out of balance, and the pressures of everyday living seem overwhelming. What's needed is a fresh perspective, a restored sense of balance . . . and God. If we call upon the Lord and seek to see the world through His eyes, He will give us guidance and wisdom and perspective. When we make God's priorities our priorities, He will lead us according to His plan and according to His commandments. God's reality is the ultimate reality. May we live accordingly.

All I'm doing right now, friends, is showing how these things pertain to Apollos and me so that you will learn restraint and not rush into making judgments without knowing all the facts. It is important to look at things from God's point of view. I would rather not see you inflating or deflating reputations based on mere hearsay.

I Corinthians 4:6 MSG

We forget that God sometimes has to say "No." We pray to Him as our heavenly Father, and like wise human fathers, He often says, "No," not from whim or caprice, but from wisdom, from love, and from knowing what is best for us.

Peter Marshall

Earthly fears are no fears at all. Answer the big questions of eternity, and the little questions of life fall into perspective.

Max Lucado

Keep life in perspective: Your life is an integral part of God's grand plan. So don't become unduly upset over the minor inconveniences of life, and don't worry too much about today's setbacks—they're temporary.

Day 83

Today's Big Question About Fellowship

Question:

What does the Bible say about your fellowship with other believers?

Answer:

You need the support and inspiration of fellow believers. There's simply no substitute for strong Christian fellowship.

If you genuinely want to become the kind of person who experiences a closer relationship with God, you'll need to build closer relationships with godly people. That's why fellowship with likeminded believers should be an integral part of your life. Your association with fellow Christians should be uplifting, enlightening, encouraging, and (above all) consistent.

Are your friends the kind of people who encourage you to seek God's will and to obey God's Word? If so, you've chosen your friends wisely. And that's a good thing because when you choose friends who honor God, you'll find it easier to honor Him, too.

So reach out and welcome one another to God's glory.
Jesus did it; now you do it!

Romans 15:7 MSG

Real fellowship happens when people get honest about who they are and what is happening in their lives.

Rick Warren

One of the ways God refills us after failure is through the blessing of Christian fellowship. Just experiencing the joy of simple activities shared with other children of God can have a healing effect on us.

Anne Graham Lotz

Brotherly love is still the distinguishing badge of every true Christian.

Matthew Henry

Be united with other Christians. A wall with loose bricks is not good. The bricks must be cemented together.

Today's Big Question About Enthusiasm

Question:

What does the Bible say about enthusiasm?

Answer:

God wants you to be enthusiastic about your faith. John Wesley wrote, " You don't have to advertise a fire. Get on fire for God and the world will come to watch you burn." When you allow yourself to become extremely enthusiastic about your faith, other people will notice—and so will God.

The stronger your faith, the better you can rise above the inevitable stresses of everyday life. And the more enthused you are about your faith, the better you can share it.

Are you genuinely excited about your faith? And do you make your enthusiasm known to those around you? Or are you a "silent ambassador" for Christ? God's preference is clear: He intends that you stand before others and proclaim your faith.

Genuine, heartfelt Christianity is contagious. If you enjoy a life-altering relationship with God, that relationship will have an impact on others—perhaps a profound impact.

Does Christ reign over your life? Then share your testimony and your excitement. The world needs both.

Whatever you do, do it enthusiastically,
as something done for the Lord and not for men.

Colossians 3:23 HCSB

Don't take hold of a thing unless you want that thing
to take hold of you.

E. Stanley Jones

We act as though comfort and luxury were the chief
requirements of life, when all we need to make us really
happy is something to be enthusiastic about.

Charles Kingsley

Your enthusiasm will be infectious,
stimulating, and attractive to others. They will love you for it.
They will go for you and with you.

Norman Vincent Peale

Your story is important: D. L. Moody, the famed evangelist from Chicago, said, "Remember, a small light will do a great deal when it is in a very dark place. Put one little tallow candle in the middle of a large hall, and it will give a great deal of light." Make certain that your candle is always lit. Give your testimony, and trust God to do the rest.

Day 85

Today's Big Question About Discouragement

Question:

When you're discouraged with the way things have turned out, what should you do?

Answer:

Don't spend too much time asking "Why me, Lord?" Instead, ask, "What now, Lord?" and then get to work. When you do, you'll feel much better.

We Christians have many reasons to celebrate. God is in His heaven; Christ has risen, and we are the sheep of His flock. Yet sometimes, even the most devout Christians can become discouraged. After all, we live in a world where expectations can be high and demands can be even higher. If you become discouraged with the direction of your day or your life, turn your thoughts and prayers to God. He is a God of possibility, not negativity. He will help you count your blessings instead of your hardships. And then, with a renewed spirit of optimism and hope, you can properly thank your Father in heaven for His blessings, for His love, and for His Son.

But as for you, be strong; don't be discouraged, for your work has a reward.

2 Chronicles 15:7 HCSB

Overcoming discouragement is simply a matter of taking away the DIS and adding the EN.

Barbara Johnson

The Christian life is not a constant high.
I have my moments of deep discouragement.
I have to go to God in prayer with tears in my eyes, and say, "O God, forgive me," or "Help me."

Billy Graham

The most profane word we use is "hopeless."
When you say a situation or person is hopeless, you are slamming the door in the face of God.

Kathy Troccoli

When things go wrong, it's easy to become discouraged. But those who follow Jesus need never be discouraged because God's promises are true . . . and heaven is eternal.

Day 86

Today's Big Question About Respecting Your Body

Question:

How does God want you to treat your body?

Answer:

It's simple (and it's important): God wants you to take care of the body He has given you. And that's precisely what you should want, too.

One of the quickest ways to wreck your world is by treating your body with disrespect.

How do you treat your body? Do you treat it with the reverence and respect it deserves, or do you take it more or less for granted? Well, the Bible has clear instructions about the way you should take care of the miraculous body that God has given you.

God's Word teaches us that our bodies are "temples" that belong to God (1 Corinthians 6:19-20). We are commanded (not encouraged, not advised—we are commanded!) to treat our bodies with respect and honor. We do so by making wise choices and by making those choices consistently over an extended period of time.

Do you sincerely seek to improve the overall quality of your life and your health? Then promise yourself—and God—that you will begin making the kind of wise choices that will lead to a longer, healthier, happier life. The responsibility for those choices is yours. And so are the rewards.

Don't you know that you are God's temple
and that God's Spirit lives in you?
1 Corinthians 3:16 NCV

A Christian should no more defile his body
than a Jew would defile the temple.
Warren Wiersbe

God wants you to give Him your body.
Some people do foolish things with their bodies.
God wants your body as a holy sacrifice.
Warren Wiersbe

God has given you a marvelous gift: your body. Taking care of that body is your responsibility. Don't dodge that responsibility! Give your body the respect it deserves.

Day 87

Today's Big Question About Negativity

Question:

What does the Bible say about negativity?

Answer:

Avoid negativity, whether you find it in others or in yourself.

From experience, we know that it is easy to criticize others. And we know that it is usually far easier to find faults than to find solutions. Still, the urge to criticize others remains a powerful temptation for most of us.

Negativity is highly contagious: We give it to others who, in turn, give it back to us. This stress-inducing cycle can be broken only by positive thoughts, heartfelt prayers, encouraging words, and meaningful acts of kindness.

As thoughtful servants of a loving God, we have no valid reason—and no legitimate excuse—to be negative. So, when we are tempted to be overly critical of others, or unfairly critical of ourselves, we must use the transforming power of God's love to break the chains of negativity. We must defeat negativity before negativity defeats us.

Let angry people endure the backlash of their own anger;
if you try to make it better, you'll only make it worse.

Proverbs 19:19 MSG

After one hour in heaven,
we shall be ashamed that we ever grumbled.

Vance Havner

Winners see an answer for every problem;
losers see a problem in every answer.

Barbara Johnson

We never get anywhere—nor do our conditions and circumstances change—when we look at the dark side of life.

Mrs. Charles E. Cowman

To lose heart is to lose everything.

John Eldredge

Negative thinking breeds more negative thinking, so nip negativity in the bud, starting today and continuing every day of your life.

Day 88

Today's Big Question About Integrity

Question:

What does the Bible have to say about the importance of integrity?

Answer:

If you want to follow in Christ's footsteps, then you must be concerned with the truth: telling it and living it.

Hey, would you like a time-tested, ironclad formula for success? Here it is: guard your integrity like you guard your wallet.

It has been said on many occasions and in many ways that honesty is the best policy. For Christians, it is far more important to note that honesty is God's policy. And if we are to be servants worthy of our Savior, Jesus Christ, we must be honest, forthright, and trustworthy.

Telling the truth means telling the whole truth. And that means summoning the courage to deliver bad news when necessary. And for some of us, especially those of us who are card-carrying people pleasers, telling the whole truth can be difficult indeed (especially if we're pretty sure that the truth will make somebody mad). Still, if we wish to fashion successful lives, we've got to learn to be totally truthful—part-time truth-telling doesn't cut the mustard.

Sometimes, honesty is difficult; sometimes, honesty is painful; sometimes, honesty is inconvenient; but honesty is always God's way. In the Book of Proverbs, we read, "The Lord detests lying lips, but he delights in men who are truthful" (12:22 NIV). Clearly, truth is God's way, and it must be our way, too, even when telling the truth is difficult.

A good name is to be chosen over great wealth.

Proverbs 22:1 HCSB

Integrity is a sign of maturity.

Charles Swindoll

Integrity is the glue that holds our way of life together. We must constantly strive to keep our integrity intact. When wealth is lost, nothing is lost; when health is lost, something is lost; when character is lost, all is lost.

Billy Graham

Take time to think about ways that you can remove yourself from situations that might compromise your integrity.

Today's Big Question About Strength

Question:

Sometimes you may feel like your strength is almost gone. When that happens, what should you do?

Answer:

If you need strength, slow down, get more rest, engage in sensible exercise, and turn your troubles over to God . . . . but not necessarily in that order.

When your world seems to be falling apart, where do you go to find strength? The gym? The health food store? The espresso bar? There's a better source of strength, of course, and that source is God. He is a never-ending source of strength and courage if you call upon Him.

Have you "tapped in" to the power of God? Have you turned your life and your heart over to Him, or are you muddling along under your own power? The answer to this question will determine the quality of your life here on earth and the destiny of your life throughout all eternity. So start tapping in—and remember that when it comes to strength, God is the Ultimate Source.

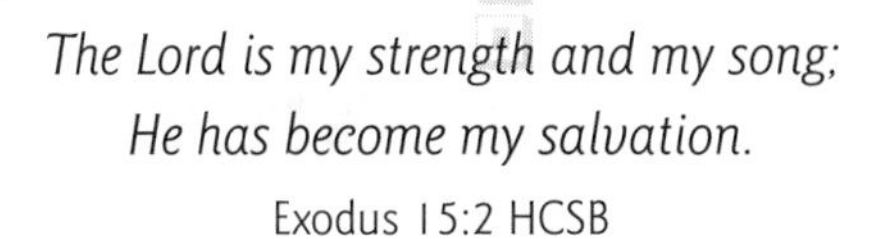

The Lord is my strength and my song;
He has become my salvation.
Exodus 15:2 HCSB

God walks with us. He scoops us up in His arms or simply sits with us in silent strength until we cannot avoid the awesome recognition that yes, even now, He is here.

Gloria Gaither

The greatness of man's power is the measure of his surrender.

William Booth

My spirit has become dry because it forgets to feed on You.

St. John of the Cross

Sometimes I think spiritual and physical strength is like manna: you get just what you need for the day, no more.

Suzanne Dale Ezell

If you're energy is low or your nerves are frazzled, perhaps you need to slow down and have a heart-to-heart talk with God. And while you're at it, remember that God is bigger than your problems . . . much bigger.

Day 90

Today's Big Question About Your Dreams

Question:

You have big dreams. What should you do about them?

Answer:

Making your dreams come true requires work. John Maxwell writes, "The gap between your vision and your present reality can only be filled through a commitment to maximize your potential." Enough said.

Are you willing to entertain the possibility that God has big plans in store for you? Hopefully so. Yet sometimes, especially if you've recently experienced a life-altering disappointment, you may find it difficult to envision a brighter future for yourself and your family. If so, it's time to reconsider your own capabilities . . . and God's.

Your Heavenly Father created you with unique gifts and untapped talents; your job is to tap them. When you do, you'll begin to feel an increasing sense of confidence in yourself and in your future.

It takes courage to dream big dreams. You will discover that courage when you do three things: accept the past, trust God to handle the future, and make the most of the time He has given you today.

Nothing is too difficult for God, and no dreams are too big for Him—not even yours. So start living—and dreaming—accordingly.

With God's power working in us, God can do much, much more than anything we can ask or imagine.

Ephesians 3:20 NCV

Set goals so big that unless God helps you, you will be a miserable failure.

Bill Bright

Allow your dreams a place in your prayers and plans. God-given dreams can help you move into the future He is preparing for you.

Barbara Johnson

Be a dreamer: Your attitude toward the future will help *create* your future. So, think realistically about yourself (and your situation), but focus your thoughts on hopes, not fears. When you do, you'll put the self-fulfilling prophecy to work for you.

Day 91

Today's Big Question About Emotions

Question:

Sometimes, negative emotions start to take control. What should you do?

Answer:

Learn to catch yourself before destructive emotions have a chance to bring you down.

Hebrews 10:38 teaches that we should live by faith. Yet sometimes, despite our best intentions, negative feelings can rob us of the peace and abundance that would otherwise be ours through Christ. When anger or anxiety separates us from the spiritual blessings that God has in store, we must rethink our priorities and renew our faith. And we must place faith above feelings. Human emotions are highly variable, decidedly unpredictable, and often unreliable. Our emotions are like the weather, only far more fickle. So we must learn to live by faith, not by the ups and downs of our own emotional roller coasters.

Sometime during this day, you will probably be gripped by a strong negative emotion. Distrust it. Reign it in. Test it. And turn it over to God. Your emotions will inevitably change; God will not. So trust Him completely as you watch your feelings slowly evaporate into thin air—which, of course, they will.

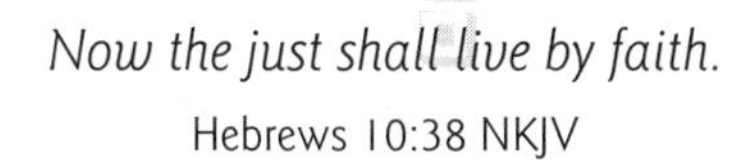

Now the just shall live by faith.

Hebrews 10:38 NKJV

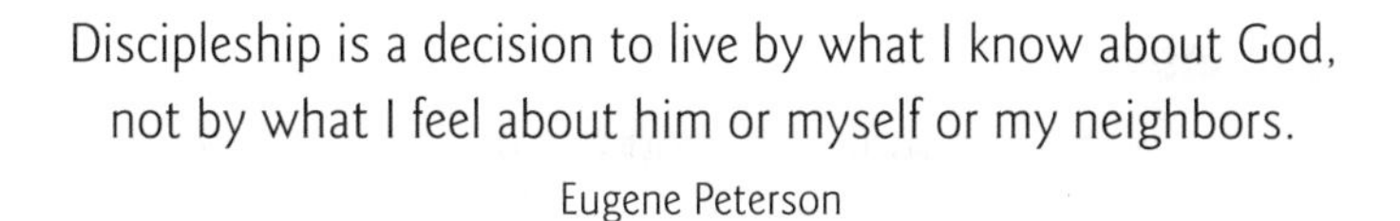

Discipleship is a decision to live by what I know about God, not by what I feel about him or myself or my neighbors.

Eugene Peterson

I do not need to feel good or be ecstatic in order to be in the center of God's will.

Bill Bright

We are to live by faith, not feelings.

Kay Arthur

Instead of waiting for the feeling, wait upon God. You can do this by growing still and quiet, then expressing in prayer what your mind knows is true about Him, even if your heart doesn't feel it at this moment.

Shirley Dobson

Here are the facts: God's love is real; His peace is real; His support is real. Don't ever let your emotions obscure these facts.

Day 92

Today's Big Question About Disappointments

Question:

Sometimes, despite your best efforts, you will be disappointed. What does the Bible say about failure?

Answer:

Failure is never permanent unless, of course, you give up and quit trying.

The occasional disappointments and failures of life are inevitable. Such setbacks are simply the price that we must occasionally pay for our willingness to take risks as we follow our dreams. But even when we encounter bitter disappointments, we must never lose faith.

The reassuring words of Hebrews 10:36 remind us that when we persevere, we will eventually receive that which God has promised. What's required is perseverance, not perfection.

When we encounter the inevitable difficulties and stresses of life here on earth, God stands ready to protect us. Our responsibility, of course, is to ask Him for protection. When we call upon Him in heartfelt prayer, He will answer—in His own time and according to His own plan—and He will heal us. And, while we are waiting for God's plans to unfold and for His healing touch to restore us, we can be comforted in the knowledge that our Creator can overcome any obstacle, even if we cannot.

Though a righteous man falls seven times,
he will get up, but the wicked will stumble into ruin.

Proverbs 24:16 HCSB

We become a failure when we allow mistakes to take away our ability to learn, give, grow, and try again.

Susan Lenzkes

If you're willing to repair your life, God is willing to help.
If you're not willing to repair your life, God is willing to wait.

Marie T. Freeman

Failure isn't permanent . . . unless you fail to get back up. So pick yourself up, dust yourself off, and trust God. Warren Wiersbe had this advice: "No matter how badly we have failed, we can always get up and begin again. Our God is the God of new beginnings." And don't forget: the best time to begin again is now.

Day 93

Today's Big Question About Putting First Things First

Question:

It's easy to get sidetracked. What should you do?

Answer:

You should form the habit of doing one thing at a time and doing things in the order of their importance. And while you're at it, please remember that setting priorities sometimes means saying no. You don't have time to do everything, so it's perfectly okay to say no the things that mean less so that you'll have time for the things that mean more.

First things first. These words are easy to speak but hard to put into practice. For busy folks living in a demanding world, placing first things first can be difficult indeed. Why? Because so many people are expecting so many things from us!

If you're having trouble prioritizing your day, perhaps you've been trying to organize your life according to your own plans, not God's. A better strategy, of course, is to take your daily obligations and place them in the hands of the One who created you. To do so, you must prioritize your day according to God's commandments, and you must seek His will and His wisdom in all matters. Then, you can face the day with the assurance that the same God who created our universe out of nothingness will help you place first things first in your own life.

Do you feel overwhelmed or confused? Turn the concerns of this day over to God—prayerfully, earnestly, and often. Then, listen for His answer . . . and trust the answer He gives.

Therefore, get your minds ready for action,
being self-disciplined . . . .

1 Peter 1:13 HCSB

Blessed are those who know what on earth
they are here on earth to do and set themselves about
the business of doing it.

Max Lucado

No test of a man's true character is more conclusive than
how he spends his time and his money.

Patrick Morley

Unless you put first things first, you're bound to finish last. And that means putting God first.

Day 94

Today's Big Question About Answering God's Call

Question:

God has a plan for everybody, including you. What does the Bible say about that?

Answer:

God is calling you to a life that is perfectly suited for you, a life that will bring happiness and satisfaction to yourself and to others.

If you really want to figure out who you are—and who you should become—it is vitally important that you heed God's call. In John 15:16, Jesus says, "You did not choose me, but I chose you and appointed you to go and bear fruit—fruit that will last" (NIV). In other words, you have been called by Christ, and now, it is up to you to decide precisely how you will answer.

Have you already found your special calling? If so, you're a very lucky person. If not, keep searching and keep praying until you discover it. And remember this: God has important work for you to do—work that no one else on earth can accomplish but you.

God chose you to be his people, so I urge you now to live the life to which God called you.

Ephesians 4:1 NCV

God wants to revolutionize our lives—by showing us how knowing Him can be the most powerful force to help us become all we want to be.

Bill Hybels

If God has called you, do not spend time looking over your shoulder to see who is following you.

Corrie ten Boom

Whatever purpose motivates your life, it must be something big enough and grand enough to make the investment worthwhile.

Warren Wiersbe

God has a plan for your life, a divine calling that you can either answer or ignore. How you choose to respond to God's calling will determine the direction you take and the contributions you make.

Day 95

Today's Big Question About The Past

Question:

If it's easy for you to stay focused on the past, what should you do?

Answer:

Remember that the past is past. So focus on the opportunities ahead of you, not the disappointments behind you.

Because you are human, you may be slow to forget yesterday's disappointments. But, if you sincerely seek to focus your hopes and energies on the future, then you must find ways to accept the past, no matter how difficult it may be to do so.

Have you made peace with your past? If so, congratulations. But, if you are mired in the quicksand of regret, it's time to plan your escape. How can you do so? By accepting what has been and by trusting God for what will be.

So, if you have not yet made peace with the past, today is the day to declare an end to all hostilities. When you do, you can then turn your thoughts to wondrous promises of God and to the glorious future that He has in store for you.

The Lord says, "Forget what happened before, and do not think about the past. Look at the new thing I am going to do. It is already happening. Don't you see it? I will make a road in the desert and rivers in the dry land."

Isaiah 43:18-19 NCV

Shake the dust from your past,
and move forward in His promises.

Kay Arthur

The devil keeps so many of us stuck in our weakness. He reminds us of our pasts when we ought to remind him of his future—he doesn't have one.

Franklin Graham

If you are God's child, you are no longer bound to your past or to what you were. You are a brand new creature in Christ Jesus.

Kay Arthur

The past is past, so don't live there. If you're focused on the past, change your focus. If you're living in the past, it's time to stop living there.

Day 96

Today's Big Question About Optimism

Question:

What does the Bible say about optimism?

Answer:

The Bible promises that if you've given your heart to Jesus, your eternal future is secure. So even when times are tough, you can be hopeful, joyful, and optimistic.

There are few sadder sights on earth than the sight of a girl or guy who has lost hope. In difficult times, hope can be elusive, but those who place their faith in God's promises need never lose it. After all, God is good; His love endures; He has promised His children the gift of eternal life. And, God keeps His promises.

Today, make this promise to yourself and keep it: vow to be a hope-filled Christian. Think optimistically about your life, your education, your family, and your future. Trust your hopes, not your fears. Take time to celebrate God's glorious creation. And then, when you've filled your heart with hope, share your optimism with others. They'll be better for it, and so will you.

For God has not given us a spirit of fear, but of power and of love and of a sound mind.

2 Timothy 1:7 NLT

The people whom I have seen succeed best in life have always been cheerful and hopeful people who went about their business with a smile on their faces.

Charles Kingsley

Developing a positive attitude means working continually to find what is uplifting and encouraging.

Barbara Johnson

Christ can put a spring in your step and a thrill in your heart. Optimism and cheerfulness are products of knowing Christ.

Billy Graham

Be a realistic optimist. You should strive to think realistically about the future, but you should never confuse realism with pessimism. Your attitude toward the future will help create your future, so you might as well put the self-fulfilling prophecy to work for you by being both a realist and an optimist. And remember that life is far too short to be a pessimist.

Day 97

Today's Big Question About Pleasing God

Question:

What does the Bible teach us about ways we can please God?

Answer:

It's simple: You can please God by obeying His commandments and by welcoming His Son into your heart.

Sometimes, it's very tempting to be a people-pleaser. But usually, it's the wrong thing to do.

When you worry too much about pleasing dates or friends, you may not worry enough about pleasing God—and when you fail to please God, you inevitably pay a very high price for your mistaken priorities.

Whom will you try to please today: God or your friends? Your obligation is most certainly not to your peers or to your date. Your obligation is to an all-knowing and perfect God. Trust Him always. Love Him always. Praise Him always. And seek to please Him and only Him. Always.

Do you think I am trying to make people accept me?
No, God is the One I am trying to please.
Am I trying to please people? If I still wanted to please people,
I would not be a servant of Christ.

Galatians 1:10 NCV

God is not hard to please. He does not expect us to be absolutely perfect. He just expects us to keep moving toward Him and believing in Him, letting Him work with us to bring us into conformity to His will and ways.

Joyce Meyer

Every day, I find countless opportunities to decide whether I will obey God and demonstrate my love for Him or try to please myself or the world system.
God is waiting for my choices.

Bill Bright

If you are burdened with a "people-pleasing" personality, outgrow it. Realize that you can't please all of the people all of the time (including your dates), nor should you attempt to.

Day 98

Today's Big Question About Service

Question:

What does the Bible say about the need to serve others?

Answer:

Whether you realize it or not, God has called you to a life of service. Your job is to find a place to serve and to get busy.

We live in a world that glorifies power, prestige, fame, and money. But the words of Jesus teach us that the most esteemed men and women in this world are not the self-congratulatory leaders of society but are instead the humblest of servants.

Are you willing to become a humble servant for Christ? Are you willing to pitch in and make the world a better place, or are you determined to keep all your blessings to yourself? The answers to these questions will determine the quality and the direction of your day and your life.

Today, you may feel the temptation to take more than you give. You may be tempted to withhold your generosity. Or you may be tempted to build yourself up in the eyes of your friends. Resist those temptations. Instead, serve your friends quietly and without fanfare. Find a need and fill it . . . humbly. Lend a helping hand . . . anonymously. Share a word of kindness . . . with quiet sincerity. As you go about your daily activities, remember that the Savior of all humanity made Himself a servant, and we, as His followers, must do no less.

The greatest among you will be your servant.
Whoever exalts himself will be humbled, and whoever humbles himself will be exalted.

Matthew 23:11-12 HCSB

In the very place where God has put us,
whatever its limitations, whatever kind of work it may be,
we may indeed serve the Lord Christ.

Elisabeth Elliot

Through our service to others,
God wants to influence our world for Him.

Vonette Bright

Whatever your age, whatever your circumstances, you can serve: Each stage of life's journey is a glorious opportunity to place yourself in the service of the One who is the Giver of all blessings.

Today's Big Question About Your Future

Question:

Sometimes, the future can be scary. What does God's Word say about your future?

Answer:

If you've given your heart to Jesus, God's Word promises that your future is intensely bright. Of course, you and your loved ones may encounter adversity and pain, but your eternal destiny is secure.

How can you make smart choices if you're unwilling to trust God and obey Him? The answer, of course, is that you can't. That's why you should trust God in everything (and that means entrusting your future to God).

How bright is your future? Well, if you're a faithful believer, God's plans for you are so bright that you'd better wear shades. But here are some important follow-up questions: How bright do you believe your future to be? Are you expecting a terrific tomorrow, or are you dreading a terrible one? The answer you give will have a powerful impact on the way tomorrow turns out.

Do you trust in the ultimate goodness of God's plan for your life? Will you face tomorrow's challenges with optimism and hope? You should. After all, God created you for a very important reason: His reason. And you have important work to do: His work.

Today, as you live in the present and look to the future, remember that God has an amazing plan for you. Act—and believe—accordingly.

"I say this because I know what I am planning for you," says the Lord. "I have good plans for you, not plans to hurt you. I will give you hope and a good future."

Jeremiah 29:11 NCV

The Christian believes in a fabulous future.

Billy Graham

We must trust as if it all depended on God and work as if it all depended on us.

C. H.. Spurgeon

Hope for the future isn't some pie-in-the-sky dream; hope for the future is simply one aspect of trusting God.

Day 100

Today's Big Question About Eternal Life

Question:

What does the Bible say about eternal life?

Answer:

God offers you a priceless gift: the gift of eternal life. If you have not already done so, accept God's gift today—tomorrow may be too late.

Okay, we've come to the end of our 100-day Q and A discussion about getting it together—and keeping it together—in a difficult world. Let's conclude by talking, once again, about the ultimate choice: your decision to establish an eternal relationship with Jesus Christ.

Eternal life is not an event that begins when you die. Eternal life begins when you invite Jesus into your heart right here on earth. So it's important to remember that God's plans for you are not limited to the ups and downs of everyday life. If you've allowed Jesus to reign over your heart, you've already begun your eternal journey.

Today, give praise to the Creator for His priceless gift, the gift of eternal life. And then, when you've offered Him your thanks and your praise, share His Good News with all who cross your path.

For God so loved the world that He gave His only begotten Son, that whoever believes in Him should not perish but have everlasting life.

John 3:16 NKJV

God has promised us abundance, peace, and eternal life. These treasures are ours for the asking; all we must do is claim them. One of the great mysteries of life is why on earth do so many of us wait so very long to lay claim to God's gifts?

Marie T. Freeman

Once a man is united to God, how could he not live forever? Once a man is separated from God, what can he do but wither and die?

C. S. Lewis

Christ is the only liberator whose liberation lasts forever.

Malcolm Muggeridge

People love talking about religion, and everybody has their own opinions, but ultimately only one opinion counts . . . God's. Think about God's promise of eternal life—and what that promise means to you.